INTELLIGENCE

ARTIFICIAL HUMAN

V/S

PUBLISHED BY DANCING ELEPHANTS PRESS

Dancing Elephants Press Publication April 2024

The front cover design was created by DR Rawson

Editors/Authors

Dr. Gabriella Kőrösi
Maryan Pelland
DR Rawson

Authors

Dr. Preeti Sigh, Lisa Prescious, Warren Brown, Libby Shively McAvoy, Dan Pelland, Leah Lynch, Annelise Lords, Gary L. Friedman, Janin Lyndovsky, Gabriela Trofin-Tatár, Buddhi Ruparathna, James Bellerjeau, Lewis Harrison, Seda Anbarcı, Phyllis Haynes, Rui Carneiro, Alison McBain, Gabriel Piemonte, Björn, Terry Day, CJ Coop

This book is organized by authors and their articles. The AI vs. HI book is a collaboration of 24 amazing authors from all over the world. It is my honor to be able to participate in this amazing project looking at Human and Artificial Intelligence together with other writers and authors in the Dancing Elephants Press Community.

Reviews

Leonard Tillerman

Have you ever worried that your coffee maker could develop a mind of its own and decide to conquer the world?

A very unlikely, yet frightening thought!

For decades, humanity has been fascinated with the concept of machines becoming more intelligent than their human overlords. Virtually transforming from the servant into the master.

It was always a far-off notion, but something fun to fantasize about. Well, in the year 2024, those days do not look quite so fantastical anymore.

If this concept has intrigued you, then the anthology, AI vs HI may be right up your reading alley!

Essentially, the book is a collection of articles, stories and poems by 24 different writers gathered from across the globe. Each one has put together passionate writing that seeks to assess and explore the unique world of AI-generated content, and its overall impact on humans.

The opinions contained within vary from outright rejection of the new, innovative technology, to those that advocate learning more about the new tool in hopes it can be used to complement, rather than replace genuine human writing.

The theme of "responsible use" rings out loud and clear throughout the entire anthology.

In short, AI is recognized as something that is not going away anytime soon. As such, human beings need to learn how to coexist with it and use the technology responsibly. Failure to do so will wipe out entire industries. Creatives such as artists and writers will have the potential to be hit the hardest.

The anthology is a balanced, intelligent and passionate analysis of the AI vs HI conundrum. The need to use these new tools with responsibility and caution comes shining through in the work. The words "proceed at your own risk" would fit nicely here!

Top marks for this one. Highly recommended!

Gary L. Friedman

Worried about all of the noise being made about Artificial Intelligence? Don't know whether to believe the hype or the apocalyptic predictions? Losing sleep over our all-too-certain dystopian future?

In this collection of essays, 24 experts from a variety of different fields provide perspective and insight into what AI is and isn't, contrasting the crucial differences of AI vs. Human Intelligence (it's more nuanced than you think), and the surprising ways they can work synergistically.

After reading this book you will come away with a level-headed, non-polarized understanding of the technologies, potential benefits to society, and the potential pitfalls we all must be aware of to steer the technology in the right direction, be it technologically or legally. (And you will be better armed to see through the marketing hype!)

Rick Allen

The greatest danger posed to creators by AI is not AI itself; it is human misuse of AI and the laziness and greed prompting that misuse. — Rick Allen, 2022

My involvement in this remarkable book is negligible. Having spent close to three decades in IT and Network Security, I witnessed the browser wars firsthand. We were assured that Google and its rivals were merely examining metadata during their web crawls. This was a lie. They were 'scraping' content and any other data they could get their hands on, all in the name of cataloging for their search engines. Their spiders or data gatherers were active 24/7, and they still are. We were even given instructions to add code to prevent our pages from being scanned by these search engines. Yet another lie.

A little more than 15 years ago, I was becoming a bit paranoid. On my own site, I hid a page from the spiders according to their instructions. I inserted many paragraphs of public domain text on that page, with a few changes to the non-essential words. I didn't change the meaning, only the wording. Within 2 years, I found those paragraphs using a Google search. The other paragraphs found did not have the changes I had planted. The concept of internet privacy seems to be a farce.

This book is not just a recommendation; it is a necessity if you have any regard for truth or integrity. Here are my thoughts on the profound insights it offers.

The profound influence of AI on human creativity and intellectual property presents us with crucial ethical and social dilemmas that demand our attention. As AI technologies, such as natural language processing, advance in their ability to mimic human speech and generate text, they also bring with them risks. One such risk is the unauthorized use of human-created content. This has already led to potential legal disputes and has put the livelihoods of creators at risk. The text underscores the immediate need for transparent and fair practices in AI development, advocating for solutions that uphold and protect human creativity and contributions. It urges readers to recognize and uphold human intelligence in the digital era.

Gabriella's voice in the narrative underscores a deep appreciation for traditional forms of storytelling, valuing the emotional depth and authenticity that come from human experiences. Celebrating the rich, longstanding tradition of storytelling that evolves from oral histories to digital writings, the text emphasizes the unique connection and understanding that human creators bring to narratives. Unlike AI, human storytellers engage with their audience profoundly emotionally, making a compelling case for the irreplaceable value of human writers.

The discussion of AI's potential unfolds within a context of ambivalence, illustrating a dystopian future where AI may dominate, reminiscent of scenarios from "The Matrix" and "The Terminator." Such portrayals serve as cautionary tales about the risks of AI surpassing human control and lacking emotional and ethical judgment. However, the narrative also recognizes the embedded role of AI in modern life, its utility in various fields, and its potential to complement human capabilities, ultimately advocating for a balance where human qualities are not overshadowed by technological advances.

The ethical quandaries continue with a focus on AI's impact on the arts, particularly concerning the rights and recognition of artists. Issues such as the unauthorized use of images and artworks by AI platforms like MidJourney and Stable Diffusion highlight significant copyright and ethical violations. The introduction of technologies like Glaze, designed to protect artists' works from being exploited by AI, underscores a growing movement toward defending artistic integrity and supporting creators to ensure they are recognized and compensated appropriately.

Echoing these concerns, the text calls for a reevaluation of the balance between technological innovation and ethical responsibility. This plea is reinforced by the seasoned perspectives of writers and artists who witness firsthand how AI can dilute the authenticity and quality of creative works. Stricter regulations and transparent practices in AI usage are necessary to protect intellectual property and ensure the sustainability of creative professions. As AI continues to infiltrate various aspects of life, the imperative grows for all involved to discern and choose responsibly between AI assistance and the indispensable value of genuine human creativity.

"Artificial intelligence is not a substitute for human intelligence; it is a tool to amplify human creativity and ingenuity." —Fei-Fei Li,

When I think deeply about AI, several words come to mind — artificial, inorganic, plastic, fake, dangerous, impersonal, disconnected, anti-human. By comparison, when I think about HI, words like creation, organic, blossoming, growth, nature, truth, heartfelt, honesty, integrity, love, and earth come to mind. — Lisa Precious

"Success in creating AI would be the biggest event in human history. Unfortunately, it might also be the last, unless we learn how to avoid the risks." — Bill Gates

This is a call for responsible technology use while respecting and protecting the rights and contributions of human artists.

Human intelligence should flourish with the human race. We don't want to underestimate the power of the physical, mental, emotional, and soulful experiences we get to be a part of. If we compromise our human interactions and hand them over to artificial intelligence, it might make tasks easier, but this story tells what the cost could be. We should build and nurture human relationships through human intelligence for a better tomorrow. — Buddhi Ruparathna

As a writer and an Artist, I have learned that our authenticity is our greatest quality. How we interact with the world through our thoughts, senses, emotions, and the deeper connection of Soul to Soul is uniquely ours.

I know a screenwriter and storyteller named Seda Anbarci, who wrote an article titled "AI Artist" Is Not a Thing/Term. Her piece didn't pull any punches. It went right to the heart of the matter.

She wrote, "You shouldn't order an article/book/poem/ or a script from AI, then post it with your name on it and call yourself a writer. YOU ARE NOT A WRITER."

RICK ALLEN, AUTHOR, Portraitist

Acknowledgment

The Dancing Elephants Book Project on Artificial Intelligence and Human Intelligence is a contemporary issue and troubling the writers who are doubtful whether their words will be taken over by AI and there are so many controversies about the efficacy of AI writing.

As an editor of Dancing Elephants Press, I would like to thank all the people who have formed a team to write the articles and contribute to the success of the book.

I would like to thank our **Chief Editor Dr. Gabriella Kőrösi** who is always ready for suggestions and new ideas.

This book was brought about mainly due to the interest shown by DR Rawson and Maryan Pelland. The decision was taken by our chief immediately to start a book. Maryan and Gabriella has worked painstakingly on this project by sending out emails and edits asking for clarification from authors.

DR has also been writing several articles on this subject.

I appreciate all the writers who have contributed to the book,

Our expert reviewers have been busy reading and reviewing all the articles and suggesting changes and giving us a feedback on our articles.

I thank Leonard Tillerman, Gary Friedman and Rick Allen who took the arduous task of reviewing the book.

Dr. Preeti Singh

Table of Contents

Preface by Maryan Pelland

Dr. Gabriella Kőrösi
Human
How Human Intelligence and Artificial Intelligence Affect Our Lives
An Interesting AI Teaching Job Opportunity..or Not
Artificial Intelligence vs. Human Intelligence in Art and Creative Writing

Maryan Pelland
Legalities vs Ethics: We're Still Arguing About AI-Generated Stuff
Lost in the Detritus — Google and Popular Authors Messing with AI
Artificial Intelligence Intelligently

DR Rawson

Artificial Intelligence vs. Human Intelligence

If You Know What Human Intelligence Is, Please Raise Your Hand

A decision Must Be Made

Dr. Preeti Singh

Exploring the Silent Oppression of AI on Our Existence
The Dynamic Relationship Between Humans and AI

Lisa Precious
AI's Inorganic Surge and the Vital Connection of Human Creativity

Warren Brown
Does AI Art Look Like Masterpieces of Famous or Popular Artists?
Annelise Lords
HI from the Heart—AI from Where?

Libby Shively McAvoy
Artificial Intelligence Cannot Replace Emotional Intelligence

Gary L. Friedman
Humans Will Need A Label
AI The Alarmists Are Worrying About The Wrong Thing

Dan Pelland
Ethical Use of OpenAI's ChatGPT
Use AI Wisely and You Might Create Enormous Benefits for Humankind

Janin Lyndovsky
Artificial Intelligence—Curse or Blessing?
Will AI Eradicate Us as an Intelligent Species?
Gabriela Trofin-Tatár
Creativity and Originality in the Context of AI vs. HI
Tales From Opposing Worlds
Buddhi Ruparathna
Let's Not Hide Those Tears

James Bellerjeau

AI-Detection Tools: Can We Uncover Who's Grifting?

Leah Lynch
Never Be Replaced
Lewis Harrison
Tips For Building & Sustaining Human Influence
Seda Anbarcı

"AI Artist" Is Not a Thing/Term

Phyllis Haynes

My secret AI Wishes
The AI Copyright Problem
We Have been Programed for AI
How To Be Human In The Age of AI

Rui Carneiro

How AI Is Tipping The scale of Job Vulnerability
AI ethics and the Dark Side of the Algorithm
AI and Deep Fake Technology: A New Threat to Human Actors
A Great Human -AI Synergy Flux

Alison McBain

Anthem for Humanity

Gabriel Piemonte

Creative AI Is Another Main Street Moment—We Should Be Concerned.

Björn

When an AI Chatbot Is a Better Conversation Partner than Humans

Terry Day
In The Writer's World – Technology and Humans make Great Gains

CJ Coop
Sentient Snark. When an AI outgrows its creators

AI vs. HI

Preface

"I believe we can change the world with one amazing book of positivity at a time." — Dancing Elephants Press founder, Dr. Gabriella Kőrösi

This book was created in support of human connection, positivity, joy, hope, and caring for each other and the environment around us. Authors of the stories, essays, and articles aim to inspire, challenge, explain, offer, and move you in a better direction. Previous Dancing Elephants Press (DEP) book projects include Holistic Journey Toward Wellness (2022), The Joy of Life (2023), Moments of Eternity (2023), and Creative Writing Ideas to Spark Your Imagination (2023).

The Beginning

A GROUP OF PASSIONATE writers, tired of AI-generated content crowding out original, meaningful writing produced by 100% human intelligence and creativity, were concerned. They came up with this 2024 book project, *Artificial Intelligence vs. Human Intelligence* (AI vs. HI).

Human writing brings creativity and joy. Our goal is to support human writers by not using AI in our writing and not providing a venue for AI-generated content. Thousands of human writers (the numbers increase every day) have pledged to use HI, or human intelligence, instead of AI in their stories, articles, and posts.

Our aims are crystal clear:

To bring global attention to the importance of HI.

To explore all aspects of AI-generated content use, its effects, and its potential impacts on humankind.

AI content impacts every human writer

EARNINGS AND COMPENSATION for human writers are eroding day-by-day, and the creative craft of writing is far less respected than it should be. That disrespect trickles down to all of us in this business of creating material for people to read, watch, and learn from.

Everywhere, we are confronted with $5.00 content hacks, artificial intelligence cheats, and new technologies that offer throwaway creative products. It's extremely challenging for skilled people to make a solid living in their creative businesses. I'm betting you're feeling it too. By staying informed and adaptable, we creatives can position ourselves as versatile, innovative makers while getting ready to navigate and embrace the future.

What you will gain from this book

YOU WILL FIND A BETTER understanding of the current creative climate. We must never abandon the idea that creative work has value. Learn how challenging it has become to make a living in creative endeavors and how you can be an activist.

Advocacy and solidarity can make a difference. There is power in standing together and fighting for better outcomes. You will come away understanding the crucial role creatives play in making content and images.

Technology is changing every industry. We'll show you how to adapt or fail. Stay informed and explore the ethical use of emerging technologies.

By staying informed and being proactively engaged, you can position yourself as versatile and forward-thinking. This knowledge will prepare you, as a human, to thrive in an art that has always sought evolving and fresh perspectives and creative approaches.

As creatives, we are, by definition, innovators. If you think about it, we tend to embrace forward progress while maintaining our efficacy in the entertainment and publishing fields. We can shape our work to meet the demands of the digital age and preserve the future of human creativity without falling prey to unethical and questionable practices.

Why We Oppose AI-generated Content

HUMANS TAMED FIRE AND learned to make tools on their own. But the technology that defined our place in nature was *human speech*, something other animals never mastered. AI can mimic human speech, but it can't supplant it.

In its development, AI large language models used a deep-learning algorithm to analyze enormous amounts of text and data to identify language patterns. So, it learned to generate responses similar in style and tone to human speech.

"all these systems do is calculate statistical probabilities of what the next word of a response should be. There's no intelligence in there at all; the system doesn't know what it's talking about – it just tries to mimic what it sees on the internet. And the more AI content floods the internet, the more the training material for future Large Language Models is either poisoned or diluted." Gary Friedman

While the development of natural language processing technologies has enormous potential, it raises important ethical and social questions. The bots scrape the entire internet for intellectual properties, regardless of copyrights and regardless of whether the material was published intentionally or re-published by bad actors seeking personal gain.

Human authors, creators, and artists did not authorize the taking and use of their properties. No one has been compensated for the use of their work, and that has enabled companies, developers, and platforms to profit handsomely. Those profiteers have never made their scraping process transparent. Lawsuits abound as creatives struggle to preserve their legal ownership rights against AI platforms.

Copyright offices and legislative bodies around the world are digging into the issues and promising solutions. They wrestle with a myriad of questions.

What are the implications of using AI-powered language models to create content? What happens to human jobs when we automate language-based tasks? How can we ensure that AI language systems give factual, unbiased, and fair responses? Can AI companies obtain training data fairly and equitably for all involved?

We want to help you stay informed and proactively engaged. This knowledge will prepare you to thrive in a world that may be falling prey to fast machine solutions without regard to quality, accuracy, or objectivity.

By taking a stand together, we can certainly meet the demands of the digital age while still protecting the future of human creativity and human contributions. There's no reason creatives shouldn't be fairly compensated and appropriately respected for their talents and skills.

AI-generated content takes readers away from human creative workers. We have enormous respect for readers who care enough to seek out the truth and support HI. In this book, we aim to give you a clear and useful perspective.

Dr. Gabriella Kőrösi

DR. GABRIELLA KŐRÖSI is a creative soul. She is passionate about Human Writing. She is an ever-evolving author, publisher, a writer, a blogger, an artist, a public health professional, a registered nurse, and a Reiki Master. She has a Master's Degree in nursing and a Doctorate Degree in Public Health, Community Health. Gabriella was born in Hungary and moved to the United States over 25 years ago and currently lives in the beautiful Pacific Northwest. She has experience in a variety of health areas including public health, addictions, mental health, nephrology, urology, cardiology, clinic nursing, disaster nursing, and community health nursing. Gabriella likes to garden, and spend time with family and friends, she enjoys picking and eating what she can grow. Gabriella loves trees and being out in nature. Gabriella's interests are focusing on positivity, creating love and joy in people's lives, and reconnecting with nature and everything around us. Gabriella loves to write and interview people about their experiences in life. Gabriella likes to create new recipes. She enjoys writing stories, writing poetry, singing, and creating art. Gabriella has published multiple books and she writes on multiple platforms. She is present on You Tube. Gabriella owns the publication Dancing Elephants Press. Website:www.gabriellakorosi.org[1].

1. http://www.gabriellakorosi.org/

Human

People with odds and magic unite.
Cells travel distances into the night.
A spark ignites when they collide.
Through division and formation, something begins.
Time and space with a hint of stardust,
Curls and bumps begin to form.
Visions of the moments speak their truth.
A child now, another human will be born.
Celebration and joy fills the air.
Struggles of learning with wonders of joy,
Will it be a girl or a boy?
Creation of life, the greatest gift.
What will happen in the span of time?
Moment to moment thoughts will form.
Creative ideas begin to emerge.
Questions and wonder open the mind.
Poems and stories fill the space.
Traditions emerge from ancestral lands.
A writer shares their innermost thoughts.
Stories form in the minds of creators.
Time to share the unique bond.
The spark that brought all of us here.
From writer to writer this is my truth.
The uniqueness of Humans rules the World.
GK 1/30/24

How Human Intelligence and Artificial Intelligence Affect Our Lives

IMAGINE A MOTHER READING a bedtime story to her child while holding a book and looking at beautiful, calming words and fun illustrations. I love stories created for children. Where the adventure begins. The love of words and stories and storytelling begins by reading and listening to books. Before books, storytelling happened by a tribal fire in a real person's words. Today, we write those stories down to share them in a book.

Once upon a time, there were humans, and then technology by humans created something else. We call this entity "AI," or artificial intelligence. I prefer the "HI," or human intelligence, part of this story. The simpler times. When people were writing down their thoughts. I prefer holding a book, reading an article in my hand, or reading online, as many forms of articles have moved online only now.

I prefer to hear a story from a human being telling me their experience. I like to be blown away by the beautiful wordplay created by a human being in poetry, while reading an essay, a true story, or a fictional creation. I prefer a being that can tell me a story that is not made up by an AI intelligence that has no idea what it means to be human.

Humanity and human writers will always be my first choices. I do not use the word *always* lightly. In this case, I am certain I always prefer human writing.

I think the way humanity can express the emotions of a lived or imagined experience is one of the most amazing gifts we have. My full intent is to support HI, HI writers, and HI creators.

I want to read writing that comes from the heart of a living being. It's as simple as that. I support human writers.

What does the future hold?

IN THE FOREST, IN A deep, secure place, people are hiding from machines. They struggle to make ends meet. Kids cannot go outside to play. They live mostly in darkness. Limited food. Fresh fruits and vegetables are almost nonexistent. Everyone is trained to fight for their lives.

They live underground. They can only come out at certain times, and they live their lives in fear of being hunted and caught by a machine. There are many movies like *The Matrix* or *The Terminator*, where artificial intelligence takes over the world and humans are trying to survive. It is the ultimate scare. Robots who do not "care" nor can they make an emotionally intelligent decision and an ethically correct decision for humanity. We watch and enjoy science fiction movies. Today we do. Will we tomorrow?

I am who I am today. The future is uncertain. Who or what will I be tomorrow?

When I think about artificial intelligence, many questions come to mind.

Do you like AI? Can part of AI be considered human as the information comes from human knowledge? Is AI good for us? Is it all bad? Where is the line in the sand when we talk about artificial intelligence vs. human intelligence? How far can we go with this? Where does humanity end and AI begin?

I prefer humanity over a machine, for certain. Yet we are getting more and more comfortable with machines. They are embedded in our lives. We use machines and technology in every aspect of our lives, from medicine to computer technology to complex remote operations in space. Technology is everywhere, and things are evolving very fast.

There are certain things in our lives where AI can be embraced and can be looked at as a blessing. We create a command, and robots learn from us, creating a new intelligence to be able to do highly sensitive research procedures, computer technology, support, and response. An example would be oncological research.

Dr. Mehmet Yiltz explains this in his article: *Practical Use of Artificial Intelligence in Oncology and Genetics (2021).*

"AI machines can independently emulate human thought patterns using deep learning algorithms and artificial neural networks made up of cascading layers of data."

We build and control machines that can go to places where humans cannot go and do tasks that humans cannot complete. I wonder how far this can go before AI technology tells humans what we can and cannot do.

How much time do we have as humans before AI starts to control our lives?

CAN A MACHINE POSSIBLY fully understand a concept, make a decision, or create an ethical answer? I do not believe so. I do believe that humanity needs to come first.

In our specific situation as writers, our work can be easily stolen from online content by a machine. The machines are plagiarising our work without our permission and without us getting any credit or payment as the original creator of the content.

Interestingly, when humans do this to another human, even by accident, they can end up in a lawsuit or kicked out of school because of plagiarism. I had a friend at school who had this situation come up. She forgot to add a reference. She was gone from the program. Yet, now here we have AI taking the work of writers and taking the jobs of humans.

I am sure part of AI technology is good; lives can also be saved with AI, and they can be destroyed.

The question is, where do we draw the line in the sand? How far are we willing to go?

Is it possible that humans will eventually become integrated with AI? Can we be part human and part AI? Would you want to be?

I know I prefer simple times. Less machine intervention. I am fine without Chat GT bots, video games, and complex machines. There is a fine line between the ethical dilemma of robots and AI deciding for a human being. Robots and AI technology can never be compared to a human's complex emotional system. An AI only knows what it is programmed to do and follows its algorithms; it probably can evolve, but not to the point of understanding what humanity in itself means.

How do you see AI in your life? What do you think this world will come to with more and more available AI technology?

References

Dr. Mehmet Yildz (2021) Practical Use of Artificial Intelligence in Oncology and Genetics. Retrieved from https://medium.com/technology-hits/practical-use-of-artificial-intelligence-in-oncology-genetics-2cf80341983

An Interesting AI Teaching Job Opportunity AI vs. HI Or not...

Life brings interesting new experiences every day. Recently, I was sharing my article on LinkedIn when a message popped up. The message was a "sponsored" job advertisement from a person named Leab Becker stating, "Flexible writing consultant opportunity."

The posting was recruiting me as a writer to go and teach AI how to write for $25 per hour with a maximum of $1000 per week. The message emphasized how I stood out as a writer and that this would be a very flexible opportunity for me; I could work from anywhere. The message stated that I could work any hours I liked from no hours to 40 hours per week.

There was an *apply now* at the bottom of the message and a statement that people with my profile can start consulting within seven days. I am certain this message comes from some type of algorithm that finds people while scanning the internet. The message also contained the fact that over 50% of people with a profile like mine end up doing the consultation and earning money.

I wondered why I got this message from a random person I do not know. The advertisement comes from a company called *Outlier*.

In their job description statement, "Outlier helps the world's most innovative companies improve their AI models by providing human feedback. In this role, you will become an AI coach of sorts, assessing the quality of AI-generated writing, reviewing the work of fellow writers, and crafting original responses to prompts to teach the model what truly excellent writing looks like."

They describe what tasks they require and how a person can teach AI. They even show a sample page where you can see an AI response and what you would be working with. Alarm bells are going through my head. *High alert.* I do not want AI to become more and more human in writing, so I could not differentiate between whether this was written by a human or a machine. The whole idea of writing for me is to show humanity and emotions. I do not care about the emotions of a machine.

Maybe I got the notice because I used #writing and #writers in my post, I am not sure. I was very surprised, and this was ironic, as we had been trying to support human writers. We were also writing a book about AI vs. HI.

Even though it could be nice to get paid more for my writing, this is, for sure, not a price I am willing to pay. I find it so ironic to hire writers to teach AI how to write, as it will ultimately decrease opportunities for writers to write.

I am happy to support humans who write, and I do. I spend many hours editing and working with writers and poets behind the scenes to support their work. As a writer, author, and publisher, I will not, however, teach AI how to write.

Artificial Intelligence vs. Human Intelligence in Art and Creative Writing

ART

Artists work hard to create something that they like, and hopefully, someone else will like their work enough to buy it one day. I enjoy art and creativity created by humans. I create art myself. I also tried and enjoyed watching the creativity for text-to-art on Canva and seeing others create magical images on different AI art platforms.

The images are imperfect, and some AI art is breathtakingly beautiful. Looking at these images, I can see which ones were created by humans and which were created by AI. I like images created by Warren Brown for his comics and poetry. You can find an article and a biography of Warren in this book.

I enjoyed creating a handful of these text-to-art images myself. It is very interesting to write down a few words from my poetry, for example, and generate an image. I could imagine using all my art and photography to enter a text and see what comes up. I wish this option would be available.

I started some research and read some articles by other writers, including Maryan Pelland and Gabriel Piemonte, talking about the artists that are now getting shortcutted because of AI images. In my research, I found there are artists who had worked very hard on their portfolios, creating images like dragons, for example, by Greg Rutkowski, only to find that their work was copied and their name was added to the image even if they did not create the image. Numerous news outlets covered this story, including Kashmir Hill's February 2023 article in the *New York Times.*

According to the *MIT Technological Review* article (2022) by Melissa Heikkilä, the images are scraped from the internet by open-source AI programs without the artist's knowledge or permission. No money or credit is given to the original artist. Other artists, including Karla Ortiz and Steven Henderson, found their work used without their permission. A website, HaveIBeenTrained.com, was launched in 2022 to help artists find out if their work is among those being taken. Platforms that use artist images without permission include and are not limited to MidJourney, Stable Diffusion, Dream Studio, LAION-5B, and the viral app LensaAI.

Glaze is a new technology that goes beyond watermarks to prevent AI from stealing and altering images from the artist's website or any other online platform. Glaze scrambles the image in such a way that AI is not able to recognize it. "Glaze is a system designed to protect human artists by disrupting style mimicry."

After reading information about how AI-generated programs stole artist's work, I am standing by artists and will not use AI-generated images in my articles and books from now on. Although it is fun, the images were taken from people who worked very hard and created amazing images. I hope that the damage can be stopped and the artists who were hurt can still get jobs and credit for their work in the future.

WRITING

To me, writing is like flowing art on a canvas. When I start, I have a hard time stopping. I can write all the time. Ideas are flowing through my brain, like rain catching the river to get a ride into our oceans. I love to write. I also believe that writers need to get credit for their work, their thoughts, and their ideas.

As a writer, I do not want to be replaced by artificial intelligence. I do not want my work to be stolen by some AI machine who wants to use my ideas and words without my consent. I think that is a very unjust, unlawful, and rude thing to do.

Throughout my nursing education and my Ph.D., it was deeply embedded in me how important it is to give credit to the people who spent their time doing research and writing articles. I cannot even imagine taking someone else's work and not giving them credit for it.

We humans can create so many beautiful things. Writing is magic. While I can choose to make some of my writing open source and available to the public, I would never agree to AI stealing my work. I would be fine with AI using my work for non-profit ideas if I got credit for it. Without asking, using someone's work is neither ethical nor legal.

I stand with the human writers fighting for their work to be preserved, credited, and compensated according to their wishes. Many writers, including myself, work very hard—many long hours of writing, editing, and formatting—for little or no compensation. Writers who use AI are taking away from writers who do their research and use their creativity to write their stories.

I am grateful to be part of this movement to support writers.

Where do you stand?

I am not against AI as a concept, as long as it is not stealing our work and is used responsibly. I don't think AI will ever replace humanity, yet it can create difficulties for humans that could be prevented and changed with appropriate planning and safeguards.

RESOURCES

glaze.cs.uchicago.edu

Maryan Pelland

MARYAN PELLAND JOYFULLY identifies as a writer/self-publisher/editor/mentor and baby boomer. She began professional writing at 16 when she convinced the editor of The (Chicago) Daily Herald to let her write and produce a weekly section for local teenagers. That may have been her boldest career with an ingrained passion for communications, and a journalism degree, she learned writing and developmental editing skills from some of the wisest (and meanest)

editors and publishers in the business. Transitioning into editing, developmental editing, and publishing, Maryan served as editor-in-chief for a weekly newspaper and then wrote for dozens of major newspapers, magazines, and websites. Her writing-related credits include a dozen books, thousands of articles and features, mentoring, teaching, and a well-circulated magazine for women.For the past ten years, Maryan Pelland has mentored burgeoning writers who want to make money writing. She writes about surviving the struggle, technology, artificial intelligence, relationships, life-challenges, and creativity. Her keen eye for detail and commitment to the craft make her a sought-after professional in the publishing world. She describes herself as an upbeat, energetic, Buddha-centric grandmother who will never get too old to engage. She dotes on her 15 grandchildren, makes pottery in her basement, and dabbles in art and photography. She doesn't love cats, seldom takes moonlight walks on the beach, and is a barrel of fun and opinions.

Legalities vs Ethics: We're Still Arguing About AI-Generated Stuff

Developing laws takes forever, but what of fairness and ethical behavior?

I've been a professional writer for more than half a century, and I can tell you how much work writing is, how easily people steal your work, and how challenging it is to make a decent living.

I've written books, newspaper stories, magazine articles, web content, marketing stuff, grants, and radio scripts. I have ghostwritten about a dozen books. I've made a great living.

My firm stance is this: A person who cannot compose a relatable, clean, supported, engaging, useful piece of writing needs to be in some other form of expression. That person is not a writer.

No AI platform or trick will ever make them into writers. If their work can't be born independent of a robot stuffed with material purloined from human creators, it is not their work and is unethical.

On writing and human creativity

SO, WE CONSIDER THE "content developer" who prompts a bot to write an article about widgets — something the particular human is not qualified to write about.

We think about the entrepreneur who sees an opportunity to scrape dry academic articles from a website and run them through a paraphrasing bot so the end product is more palatable and "written" for a 5th-grade audience.

The bot uses a database crammed with the work products of human creatives who did not give permission and were not compensated. Then the AI platform and the individual prompting the bot make money, but the writer or illustrator does not.

The human involved may vet the material or claim to. But does that person have the knowledge, the experience, or the research skills and tools to verify what the bot cranks out? Does that person understand what a primary source is when writing factual prose? What qualifies this person to sell such work and affix their name to it? Are these products plagiarized?

A court would have to determine that. To date, in the EU and the US, qualifying to register a copyright requires proof that a work was substantially made via human creativity—and writing a prompt does not suffice. The applicant must disclose to what degree the work was impacted by AI generation. Do you think applicants are being truthful about this?

On any writing platform, in any publication, in any classroom setting, it is not unlikely to find AI-generated or "paraphrased" content lurking in the shadows.

In any ten stories, at least one is not 100% human creativity. There are, for example, many stories that seem fairly well written, but it's obvious that the writer has not much background in the topic.

One comes to mind: a biographical sketch I saw of Amelia Erhardt by a 20-year-old writer whose first language is not English. It's a dull but not terrible story, and the language seems polished. The "author" posted several similar pieces daily and bragged about his income.

The writer's responses to comments on the stories are, however, written by someone with a tenuous command of English. The writing was not human writing.

Ethics vs. legalities—are we seeing talent and skill or just exploitation?

FOR ME, IT ISN'T AS much about legalities as about ethics and understanding how these AI platforms are developed.

In 2022, as all of the big ones were being launched, anything available on the web, whether copyrighted or not, was used to force-feed the databases, like geese for fois gras.

- No authors, artists, or other creatives had an opportunity to opt-out.
- Writing was just vacuumed up and used as the basis of huge windfall profits for the AI industry.

If you listen to the Copyright Office webinars from last spring, participating creators almost immediately found the demand for their work decreased sharply, and the demand has not recovered. Small publishers went out of business because they could not compete with the avalanche of AI-generated material.

Back in the early 21st century, freelance writers could make a very decent living working for publications and websites. Then, offshore content mills sprouted everywhere, paying writers pennies per hour to churn out barely literate stuff. Established writers had to compete with hacks in a boiler room who churned out poor-quality but really cheap content for around $5 per 1000 words.

Freelance writing, for 15 years or more, became an impossible way to make a living. Writers like me had to reinvent their processes and clientele to survive. The market slowly recovered to some extent as clients learned that their reputations suffered.

Then came the winter of 2022. The world went nuts for artificial intelligence, and platforms sprang up everywhere. Now, anyone can provide any content they wish by riding the backs of every writer whose work has been dumped into databases. Everyone is now "creating" something with AI.

I call your attention to the hundreds of opportunists who are more than happy to help you make thousands of dollars a month, even if you lack experience or skill, by simply feeding prompts to AI platforms and selling the results as your own work.

Those "mentors" make a fortune charging others for the "secrets." I expect they're happy to share a bit of their windfall with the AI platform of their choice. Win, win. Lose (for the creative worker).

What's the solution?

FOR NOW, THERE ISN'T one. There are too many people eager to convince themselves that producing writing or images that are not the product of their skill or talent or intellect is fair use.

Laws are coming. The EU AI Act now requires that generative AI like ChatGPT comply with transparency requirements:

- Designing the model to prevent it from generating illegal content
- Publishing summaries of copyrighted data used for training
- Disclosing that the content was generated by AI

Most AI platforms do not comply with such regulations, especially the second one.

There are numerous lawsuits pending in the US and EU against every one of these AI platforms, from Open AI to Google to Github and Microsoft.

On every publishing and content venue, this is a complex and serious issue that has made a lot of money for people exploiting a process they don't understand. These folks call themselves writers and illustrators while they game the entire industry. But they'll tell you with an ingenious demeanor that they only seek to disseminate information to everyone and make the world a better place.

But what they're providing isn't their work product. It's opportunism at best.

Lost in the Detritus — Google and Popular Authors Messing with AI

AI-Generated Content vs Human-Generated Content: Impact on Humans

I recognize the critical nature of the AI-generated content vs. human-generated content debate. The outcome, what we collectively decide to do with AI, will impact every writer, editor, content developer, and illustrator on the planet, and you must keep aware of the direction it's all moving.

This article will explore a Google project assigning several writers to crank out AI-written stories, for better or worse. Oddly, not much is being said about the project, and maybe that makes it a fail.

Google says Wordcraft is "a multidisciplinary team...that explores the human side of AI by doing fundamental research, building tools, creating design frameworks, and working with diverse communities."

AI-generated content vs. human-generated content and Wordcraft

In late 2022, Google, along with everyone else on Earth, came up with a tool for writing stories with AI. They dubbed it *Wordcraft*. They launched it with a splashy website full of marketing speak and stories by fiction writers you have probably heard of. Then it got quiet.

The URL changed, the marketing speak toned down, and there was an interesting lack of chatter about the whole thing. Wordcraft became an app that nobody ever heard of.

Nothing mind-blowing here. There is an AI story writer on every street corner these days. This particular platform is underpinned by an in-progress large language model, LaMDA (by Google, of course).

LaMDA is a machine trained to predict the most likely next word when processing a human-written prompt. But Google is all excited, claiming LaMDA self-learns higher-level ideas as it works. Experts everywhere are exploring this concept and an "emergent capability" called in-context learning. These ideas don't mean machines are taking over the world or human creativity will be supplanted. If you're worried that will happen, you should know that AI is not a consciousness.

If you've been playing around with AI generators, you are aware that prompt writing and AI output are, at least for the moment, temperamental, unreliable, inconsistent, and funky. Google says they built it to explore how a well-considered user interface could push outputs "to empower writers by giving them access to these state-of-the-art tools." Hmm.

So they paired *Wordcraft* (referred to disingenuously as a *text editor*) with a baker's dozen authors to produce a collection of short stories. The collection comes with a disclaimer:

"The writers featured here have used Wordcraft along with their own creative vision and have not authored these stories under any sort of explicit guidance or instruction."

Are the stories any good?

I surely noticed issues common to other AI-assisted writing, but not to a tremendous extent. Most pieces read comfortably. For us, none were OMG fantastic. CNET.com said, "Stephen King needn't be shaking in his boots just yet, though."

Some stories were entertaining and engaging. Many were quite clever. The author's comments are quite interesting. We've reached out to this group of writers, inviting any and all to comment on their experience, but so far have had no takers. One declined, one said it wasn't worth his time, most others didn't respond.

Android Central noted that the bot balks at prompts leaning toward harmful or hurtful acts, which could be a serious censorship issue for writers. Imagine George Orwell without hurtful scenes. But overall, the project could perhaps be described as an innocuous experiment. Interesting, but not compelling. So far, the writers involved do much better without AI input or output.

Does AI-generated content vs. human-generated content end in a creative apocalypse?

Not at the moment, though who can predict the future? For now, the most significant downside of AI-generated content vs. human-generated content is twofold.

1. A complete deluge of garbage is being dumped into self-publishing platforms, websites, print publications, and traditional publishers' platforms. This junk is churned out by get-rich-quick hacks who have never written a sentence in their lives but see a golden opportunity to toss tons of stuff against a wall so something will stick. I point to 10,000 monkeys on 10,000 typewriters for 10,000 hours — maybe a best-seller results. The sad part is, according to recent forums with the Copyright Alliances, small traditional publishing houses are closing their doors partially because of this trend.
2. Talented writers struggle to make their work visible. There are tens of thousands of books, ebooks, and whitepapers spammed onto self-publishing platforms every day. Opportunistic writers crank out multiple books a day with no attention to quality. Legitimate crafters spend more and more time marketing and promoting their work and less time writing.

It's becoming problematic to register copyrights since the U.S. Copyright Office is mired in the AI-generated content vs. human-generated content battle and struggles to determine what is human creativity and what is not. I have heard of authors who had registered copyright only to have it canceled because of AI-generated content vs. human-generated content issues.

Are we in deep doo-doo creatively?

Talk to a dozen creatives, and you'll hear a dozen or more opinions. The world is, at this moment, not in a creative crisis, but things are moving quickly. Apparently, the U.S. Copyright moguls will conclude that the amount of human input in a project will determine whether or not the project is copyrightable. Good luck to them figuring out how to prove that ratio.

There are rising numbers of job board editing and writing opportunities with these notations.

1. Do not apply for this job unless you are up to speed on AI-generated writing platforms and prompts.
2. Do not apply for this role if you use AI-generated writing in any form to produce your work.

A growing number of content-driven websites are obviously using AI, so it's more difficult for humans to land some jobs. However, the upside is that the more AI-centric the content is, the lower the quality of writing. It becomes repetitive, cold, generic, and recognizable from a long way off. So, these companies may decide to return, at least partially, to a human component if they want their property to compete long-term.

What happens next for human writers and illustrators?

We will adapt. I can, so far, spot an AI image a mile away. I can probably tell you what platform generated it. For me, there is a time and place to use AI illustrations. Users should always disclose such origins. Illustrators will learn to craft creative prompts that output much higher-quality art than the drivel being passed around currently. Yes, we will adapt and expand our thinking

Writers and authors can save a lot of time right now by employing certain AI writing skills. Editing can be automated to a degree. I mean, who needs to spend a day correcting comma splices? ChatGPT is great at brainstorming article ideas or plot ideas. AI saves a ton of time in making outlines and concept lists. I use ChatGPT to set up my workflow.

Still, humans must keep their eye on these bots (and their over-zealous creators) and keep abreast of the news in this space. In the meantime, humans—keep writing, keep illustrating, and be happy.

Artificial Intelligence Intelligently

Is AI the Devil's Spawn? Not if HI and Common Sense Prevail

Artificial intelligence is not new. 1950: Alan Turing published Computer Machinery and Intelligence about machine intelligence, called The Imitation Game. Two years later, Arthur Samuel wrote a checkers program for an IBM 701 prototype. Once known as the defense calculator, the 701 was IBM's first commercial computer offering.

AI has a long and complicated history, which spawned AI-generated content platforms just about a year ago. In late 2022, large language model companies unleashed AI-generated writing and illustration platforms on the world. Humans, delighted by a glittering new toy, jumped on the technology and began hurling obscene amounts of money at Open AI and MidJourney.

Humans, intelligent or not, went crazy for the technology without much investigation, evaluation, or prudent thought. Everyone was "writing" and "illustrating" via a proliferation of platforms that coughed up hairballs from the get-go. In under 60 days, you couldn't find anyone who hadn't heard of or tried artificial intelligence toys allegedly built on the backs of hard-working human writers and artists.

As a trained, experienced human writer and artist of an advanced age, I am not a fan of "creative" work performed by zeros and ones. But I don't think of artificial intelligence as the spawn of the devil, nor do I think it will be the ruination of mankind. But we need to take a beat and take a close look at how chatbots need to be constrained to not violate the rights of human intelligence.

Tech experts say the more we automate, the more we need human workers to supervise, provide authentic scrutiny, and interpret the insights. That makes it more essential to keep human intelligence (HI) in AI.

Artificial intelligence economics

Marketsandmarkets.com says the global artificial intelligence software market (other than generative AI platforms, which will add $55 billion) was valued at $64 billion USD in 2022, $150.2 billion in 2023, and is projected to grow to more than $300 billion in five years. Revenue forecast? Conservatively, $1,345.2 billion. The largest market in 2023 was the US.

This technology provides a large number of jobs at all levels, from entry to top jobs, and there is a high demand for applicants. Entry-level AI engineers make around $118,166 annually, with steady increases. Engineers with three to five years of experience command salaries in the neighborhood of $150K.

College degrees are not always required. Technical schools abound, apprentice-type jobs are possible, high schools are adding AI training programs all the time, and experience in other tech fields translates to AI pretty well. This is not a terribly bleak picture. AI technology in various industries also expands the need for certain support workers.

Moravec's paradox says that contrary to traditional assumptions, reasoning requires very little computation, but sensorimotor and perception skills require enormous computational resources.

AI—the good, the bad, and the miraculous

If we apply AI to nothing else, adding it to our healthcare toolbox was, is, and will be nothing short of miraculous. Artificial intelligence is behind machines that can detect diseases and identify cancer cells. AI makes early diagnosis more accurate, so dangerous conditions and diseases may become a problem of the past. AI identifies new drug possibilities.

Recently, I was diagnosed with cancer, and an AI powered robot removed every trace of the tumor from my internal organ in about 40 minutes through four one-inch incisions. I had no post-surgical pain and recovered in remarkable time. An AI scan scoped all of my organs to rule out the possibility of any other growth.

Currently, AI is identifying the structure of every protein in every substance. Once, it took a decade to explore fewer than a dozen protein compositions. This year, AI has cataloged more than two million, paving the way for incredible discoveries and solutions. (https://www.cnet.com/science/biology/googles-deepmind-ai-predicts-3d-structure-of-nearly-every-protein-known-to-science/)

Artificial intelligence, governed by careful and prudent human intelligence oversight, is making an impact in nearly every industry. Here are just a few:

Navigation and transportation
Gaming and entertainment
Education
Security and threat prevention
Finance
Agriculture
Astronomy
Archaeology
Manufacturing
Homelife

For now, the ugly part is the AI-generated content segment, which is about as organized, understood, and rational as the Wild West. I'd be hard-pressed to think of another new product that was as blindly accepted and exploited as these platforms have been over the past year. Everyone seems to have lost their minds and maybe their sense of ethical behavior because chatbots are fun, shiny, and accessible.

We see students at almost every level, from primary grades to universities, churning out assignments as if the learning component has no merit. Content developers have dumped tons of half-assed "writing" and imagery on the web. People argue about why it's perfectly ok to use material that was, in all likelihood, cobbled together from material created by humans who have had no say in how it's used.

Until the tsunami slows, it might be prudent to proceed with caution if you choose to avail yourself of chatbots and text-to-image platforms. No matter how you frame a prompt to secure an image or a story, work created by uncompensated humans and used without permission plays into the response your prompt receives. Even if you don't specify "in the style of" a certain artist in your prompt, HI contributed to the database that churns out an image. You did not create it. You can't copyright it. You may wish to consider the big picture.

In any case, the question of responsibly and ethically using AI to the advantage of HI is vast and complicated. It will be a while before we refine the technology, if we ever do. Each of us needs to be aware of the ramifications of our own actions, and it's in our own best interests to keep abreast of developments on all fronts.

DR Rawson

THE PICTURE IS OF THE author from the Rawson Business Archives.

I WAS HOMELESS AS A boy, from nine and a half to thirteen years of age. We were poor, and our food came from some of the most popular Italian restaurants in town. I was the head of household for my mother, brother, and two sisters. My mother was twenty-seven when we became homeless, and she had never worked.

My schooling was the best. Primary grades were in an all-Hispanic school. My sister and I were the only blond-haired, blue-eyed children.

In middle school, we moved into the heart of San Diego, and our school was all African-American, except for my sister and me.

High school was more mixed-race and provided another opportunity to learn. I did well in school and was prepared to attend Rutgers University in New York on a full scholarship. The other two colleges were the same. They wouldn't let me in because of my parents' lack of willingness to cooperate with the school.

I went into the Air Force, Vietnam, and back to Southern California.

Through an unusual set of circumstances, ten companies backed me so that I could start my first company in Florida. I was on the high side of twenty-one. The stocking manufacturer's representative business became extremely successful in fourteen months, and I sold it. At twenty-three, I bought the company I went to work for. It was a company that manufactured cranes, hoists, and other equipment used in overhead lifting.

I sold that company to the employees three years later. A pattern and a way of life emerged. I started, purchased, or took over twenty-seven companies from when I was twenty-one until I retired by selling my last business at age seventy-five.

Writing

A long-time friend, former employee, and entrepreneur, Gary L. Friedman[1], suggested that I start writing. He thought I could share stories of my travels, adventures, knowledge, and wisdom that I had gained over the years. That was October 2021.

I've published a few books** and written over four hundred articles today. These are available at my library by clicking here[2]. My personal website is ww.DRRawson.com[3].

---

1. https://www.friedmanarchives.com/
2. https://www.drrawson.com/my-library
3. http://www.drrawson.com/

** UnLikely, my memoir, Meet Carlo Chappman, a novel, Meet Taylor Richards, a novel, Story Book I, a children's book, Story Book II, a children's book, and Story Book III, a children's book.

No AI was used to write this story. It's all human intelligence. DR

Artificial Intelligence vs. Human Intelligence

And so it begins. Unlike the battle of the bands, this battle of AI vs. HI is something that will likely have a far-reaching effect on writing and even the meaning of what it means to be a writer of anything. Let's say that today you turn 35, 45, or 55 years old. Please tell me what you think the impact of AI will be on writers in 5, 10, 15, or 25 years from now. "You can't" is the answer you're looking for; no one can tell us.

What do these have in common?

THE AUTOMOBILE, TELEPHONE, ballpoint pen, telex, computers, atomic fusion, R-19, television, digital, mobile phones, compression algorithms, the Internet, the dark web, satellite, Hubble, visitation to other planets, baud, bursty, dot com, encryption, and AI (they are not in perfect order).

These are technological advances. There are literally hundreds of thousands of new discoveries, inventions, and paradigm shifts that have occurred since the time of the US Civil War. What preceded all of the technologies listed? Human Intelligence (HI).

Now what?

THE REAL ANSWER IS that we don't know. A scientist working at Texas Instruments worked on a team to develop the largest computer storage size possible, given the size constraints of the popular tape memory drive. They wanted to be the first to reduce computing costs by increasing the storage medium's size.

After months and months, there was the announcement, and at TI headquarters, a celebration was held in order to celebrate the achievement of creating the world's first 10 Mb (megabyte) tape storage for computers.

My friend and brother Mason told me this story after I had discussed becoming the new president and CEO of one of the first Internet service providers in Southern California. I asked, "How long did that achievement and computer milestone stand?" His answer:

"Just under 30 days."

I was privileged to be included in many early discussions about privacy on the Internet. I was there when the first VOIP (Voice over Internet Protocol) contract was signed, for example. Each of these milestones had intended and unintended consequences. Those of us who were trying to figure it out did okay, but maybe not the best job. I think that given the resources and the pressures at that time, we did an outstanding job.

In each case, thousands of voices were heard. There was no shortage of opinions. The important thing is that in each case, each voice mattered.

This book's intent is to explore AI as it impacts our lives, especially in the writing and art spaces. What will be the impact of AI? We'll look at many aspects of its existence and impact presently and into the future.

Do you have an opinion? I do. Many of these technologies and inventions have happened on my watch. Some have had my direct involvement. As a result, I haven't grown horns, nor do I speak with a forked tongue. But I have the benefit of experience as I evaluate any new spreading technology.

Many of us, as writers, are concerned about having our work compared to and competing with AI-generated writing. We rely on

HI (human intelligence), and we encourage you to consider doing the same. Let's not cave to the easy way—we're creative, thoughtful people who have the power to disseminate information. We are who we are. Please decide not to use AI-generated writing.

And one last thought, what about the children? Our cause is just, but who's fighting for the children? Who is going to ensure that what they read isn't just drek that was mass-produced to provide something so children have books? Will future generations miss out on the literature created by humans because it has been replaced by cheaper AI-generated texts?

Every school board in America should be issuing statements against AI in education, especially in the lower grades when children lack the skill to discern and take so much on pure belief.

Communication is the key, and we're communicating. The more you know, the more meaningful the HI movement is to everyone.

If You Know What Human Intelligence Is, Please Raise Your Hand

No, really, have we given this our best thought?

Well, now we have proof. An MRI proves conclusively that someone has a brain. Is that helpful? No. Why? Studies show that nearly every one of us was born with a brain. Studies also show that not nearly enough of us use it when necessary.

Personal Story

I WOULD BE SKINNING a rabbit and trying to do my best, but I would make a wrong move. My dad would look over at me and say, "Have you thought about using your brain for something besides a hat rack?" Oops.

My wife and I have six grown children, and I still wonder: "I know they have a brain, but do they use it? When it's needed?" You can guess about that.

TODAY

WE'RE FOCUSED ON AI vs. HI. AI is becoming more and more obvious and ubiquitous. In preparing for this story, I ran across this ad: (***need to insert the image here***)

That's a no-brainer, as they say. We've already proven that in a number of industries or verticals, there's money to be saved. But we're writers and readers of what we hope is good writing. My question is, can AI actually write a better story than a writer using their HI—human intelligence?

Is it an equal playing field?

MOST WOULD SAY, "NO, it's not."

However, this writer says, "I think it is." AI does exactly what it was intended to do at the expense of our fellow writers over decades. It provides content. If you want content, AI might be your best answer. I doubt it. But, hey, I'm not you.

My money is on the writer using their human and emotional intelligence to give me a story, article, blog post, or comment using informed consciousness. Some writers are geniuses; you can tell from the way in which their material is presented. That's great.

Some writers, like my rocket scientist friend, Gary L. Friedman, can take the most intricate details and reduce them to a few sentences anyone can understand. It's a gift.

Others of us have thoughts and ideas we feel compelled to share. For example, that's the way I'm writing to you now. How could any machine come across with passion and understanding spanning seventy-seven years and have traveled as I have? No AI will not have felt the love, frustration, anger, and calm I've felt from people all over the world.

This is why human intelligence is so important. As writers, we come from different places, each with a point of view that gives us the fire, passion, and desire to share our stories.

As I understand it, AI can't provide content without spelling out a use case, and then someone (with a brain and some level of intelligence) tries to describe what they want in X number of words. AI does not think; it responds to human intelligence. Isn't that a kick? It responds to ***human intelligence.***

After traveling and meeting people from so many different cultures and different backgrounds, I can honestly say I've never met someone who didn't possess human intelligence. Everyone is different, but so is everyone's perspective. That means that two people can experience something on the same subject and arrive at two different conclusions. I love that. It's not canned. It's not just content.

Call to action

PLEASE DON'T SELL YOURSELF short. You don't need AI to do what you've always done as a writer. You've written from your perspective with the knowledge that you have or have found and discerned for the reader. YOU ARE IMPORTANT to us readers. We want to understand the world through your eyes, with your intelligence.

PLEASE DO NOT SUCCUMB TO AI. You are so much more than enough. As writers and artists, give us your best; as readers, demand the best. That's all we're asking.

A Decision Must Be Made

Going forward, AI will absolutely be in our lives. Will you use it to write?

Each new day brings its own set of challenges, but some of our decisions are so basic. For example, most of us wear clothes and brush our teeth daily. We were taught that, but we decided to continue those choices.

CHOICE

Often, the things we do or don't do all boil down to a decision made on an impromptu or sudden basis. Some choices are well thought out, taking days or weeks to arrive at a choice that suits you, your personality, and your belief systems.

Research often comes into play. As a retired CEO, all my business decisions of consequence came with research. It was either my own work or that of someone I trusted within our organization. I needed the research to broaden my understanding of the problem at hand before making the decision.

In 2023 and now 2024, so many articles have been written on writing. How to, when to, what to, where to, and even why to write are often the topics of articles, blogs, or stories.

TRUST

We expect that we can trust what is being written in the news, non-fiction, poems, and other works. Why shouldn't we? Our expectations come from literally centuries of reading. If anyone has ever tried to write, they get a glimmer of all that goes into creating any non-fiction or fiction piece. It has always come from the mind or minds of the author or authors.

As we progress in this century, the problem becomes, can we trust what we're reading?

How do we know the writer wasn't using artificial intelligence (machine learning, aka AI) to research the topic? What if AI hallucinates (a fancy term for "lies") or gives us misleading information? If it's used in the research, can we trust what is being offered as a result?

If we're not given correct information, it's a case of "garbage in, garbage out." This is a standard form of recognition within the computer programming community. It should also be within the writing community as well.

Let's get back to the concept of choice.

If you're a writer and you're using AI-generated content to explain or identify a problem, how do you know that you can trust the result? You should have come to the same conclusion as this:

You Can't

Therefore, you will have to use your resources to ensure its accuracy. So, what decision will you make about using AI in your writing? Has AI become part of who you are? Or are you still using your own human intelligence (HI) to discern and write about important or requested topics?

When you make a choice, if you have moral character and integrity, then the decision becomes your position. If you take the position that you will not use AI in your writing (regardless of the reason), then you've also taken a position. Are you right or wrong?

You have either decided to use AI or you haven't.

OPTIONS

The thought crosses one's mind that there may be exceptions. Really, like what? Humor pieces? Fluff pieces, works of fiction. My answer is NO. Suppose you've made the decision not to use AI to create content. Then that's your decision. I hope you'll do exactly that.

A CAUTIONARY TALE

Please indulge me for just a minute. For years, I watched as people committed to attending a particular event. It was recurring every week.

The first week, fresh from their commitment, they would attend and seemed to really enjoy everyone's company and the whole experience.

The next week, they would attend again. By the third week, they would get out of bed, check the weather, and go back to bed if it didn't suit them. Commitment lost. The next week was a sunny day and looked really easy. Commitment won. And so it would go; every week was a new decision. There really wasn't a commitment. Here's the reason. A decision was made every week based on what suited them. If it looked like stormy weather or was difficult, there would be no commitment. If it was a beautiful and wonderful day, let's say an easy one, then there was a full commitment.

Is that the way you want to live your life?

FINALLY

I know a screenwriter and storyteller named Seda Anbarci, who wrote an article titled *"AI Artist" Is Not a Thing/Term*[1]. Her piece didn't pull any punches. It went right to the heart of the matter.

She wrote, *"You shouldn't order an article/book/poem/ or a script from AI, then post it with your name on it and call yourself a writer. YOU ARE NOT A WRITER."*

Honestly, all I can add to that is **amen.**

---

1. *https://medium.com/dancing-elephants-press/ai-artist-is-not-a-thing-term-cd0eadce12b3*

Dr. Preeti Singh

I AM DR. PREETI SINGH. I am a professor. I have been in the academic sphere for five decades. I am currently involved in creative writing. I am an editor for some online publications. My two main places of work in education have been at Jesus and Mary College (University of Delhi) and Jagannath International Management School (JIMS) Kalkaji where I was Head Post Graduate Department of International Business Management.

I was also Managing Editor of Journal 8M (The Indian Journal of Management and Strategy). I have worked in a corporate organisation and have also been an entrepreneur in the fashion business owning a boutique. As an educationist, I have been associated with many post graduate and undergraduate institutes in Delhi University and Management Institutes. I have participated in National and International conferences as an organiser, paper presenter, discussant, Keynote speaker, and Chairperson in India and abroad.

I have presented research papers in Sweden, Germany, U.S.A., Canada, and Thailand, at conferences and delivered special lectures at foreign universities. I have conducted the Faculty and Management Development Programme. I have a large number of published research papers, articles, and book reviews in management journals. I have also received the Best Paper Award.

My well-known books in the area of finance are Investment Management, Portfolio Management, Fundamentals of Financial Management, Dynamics of Indian Financial System, and Stock and Commodity Markets. My other interests are in issues relating to 'Human Resources Management', 'Culture and Economic Development, Nature & environment' and 'Women, and Work in the Urban Space'.

During COVID-19 I gave up full-time work but professors never retire so I have some appointments and commitments to teaching, evaluating, and mentoring.

Currently, I am on the governing board of a Charitable Eye Institute where I am doing honorary service. I am also an advisor and mentor to a start-up, named Young Mindz which is an online educational platform. I am interested in wellness, I engage with people. I love to sing and dance. I enjoy doing yoga every day and love my nature walks. I enjoy reiki. I am a trained teacher and practitioner in reflexology.

I live, love, and laugh and I treat each day of my life as a special gift.

Exploring the Silent Oppression of AI on Our Existence

She was sitting behind the counter, all frustrated. The AI calculator had stopped working. She could not calculate, and it was a simple addition. She was distraught. People were breaking the queue and pushing each other because she took so much time to make a bill. I went up to her from the queue and asked her if she needed help.

"No mam! My father will just come and prepare the bills. He can count and make bills manually, but I am used to an AI calculator and need a computer to prepare a bill and make the payment," she said. "You see, my dad is old school, and can do these things, but the modern generation needs faster equipment."

Was she giving her father a proud moment, or was it a disparaging remark about his being old and rusty? I did not understand. I told her that her old school dad was better than the new generation because he could think for himself. He was not completely dependent on a machine.

This made me think of technology and the changes that have come into our lives in the present time. We are so content that something else does the work for us. We want a GPS in our lives for our mind and body.

Slavery of our mind

I HAVE AMPLE EXAMPLES to show that our minds are slaves of AI.

1. If we want to go somewhere from home, then we completely rely on GPS. The GPS says to turn left, and we obey and turn left.

We just do not use our minds for directions anymore.

We have lost time, distance, and direction to think for ourselves.

2. How many of us remember the phone numbers of people? I used to remember all my friend's numbers. I used to note them, but I never needed to refresh my memory by checking my diary.

Today, if you ask me to tell someone's number, I will just not remember it, except perhaps my own phone number. I just rely on my phone to store my friend's and contact numbers, and I directly press the name, and the call begins.

Many of my friends are not even embarrassed to say that they don't remember their own phone number. I am sometimes shocked to hear it.

3. AI also controls our sleep. Even that does not belong to us. We now know when we had deep sleep, dreams, or light sleep. Who tells us? The watch that we wear. Sleep is also not our own. It has controlled our minds.

4. With the advent of generative AI, most people have stopped thinking and are writing corporate letters and articles from the suggestions of AI. Images are also made through AI. The human form and beauty of writing from the author's heart cannot be seen. The art of the artist is lost.

Am I using my mind? Certainly not. I am a slave to a technological tool, and my mind does not think at all.

Our physical slavery

WE ARE BECOMING SLAVES to AI physically as well. Let us see how.

1. Most of us have an Alexa or a Siri at home that takes over our physical activity.

Hey, Alexa switch off the lights, and there it goes and does it. I just touch a button. I am so happy. I don't have to go anywhere.

How healthy is this? With a lack of physical activity, we are only putting on weight and then taking time to shed all that weight by going on a diet or going through surgeries and medical procedures to lose weight.

What a senseless game this is, and we do not think about it.

2. We are slaves to robots too, We bought a cleaning robot. Phew, it has saved us time and physical labor, but we have also become lazy. We have lost our balance of physical activity and continue to sit all the time.

3. We use a remote to open and close doors, switch on the TV, and open locks without moving. This is such a health hazard.

4. We have stopped going to buy groceries. With the push of a button, we order everything, including food, so we do not do anything but sit in one place without moving our bodies.

What are the takeaways?

1. We should not depend completely on AI, or we will not have any physical and mental capabilities left. The human mind is always superior and can direct AI so it should not become inferior to it.
2. AI sometimes leads you down the wrong path when you use it for directions. Hence, the human mind should always reason and make judgments and fall into the trap of AI. I remember once I had to go to someone's house, and I followed the GPS, which took me 15 miles away from the destination. Sometimes it does not give proper and accurate information, and you keep on spending time looking for your location while the location is just around you and you don't even know about it.
3. Security surveillance and AI cameras impact your privacy and freedom of movement, so you should use them with care.

4. You should not be a slave to the AI because it curtails your physical movement and health issues such as cholesterol, hypertension, loneliness, and depression that set in with little or no physical activity.
5. We must be careful of ethical issues while using AI because various lawsuits are pending now for encroachment of other people's work, especially in copying writing work and images. Writers and artists are aware of these situations.

CONCLUSION

AI is not a bad thing. It is the development of technology and tools that has made our lives easy and comfortable. We have to form a balance between AI and the human mind to have a healthy and happy future. The human mind is superior, so we should give it power rather than take away its power and use AI for everything. We must exercise our brains and challenge them to support us.

"Artificial intelligence is not a substitute for human intelligence; it is a tool to amplify human creativity and ingenuity." —Fei-Fei Li,

The Dynamic Relationship Between Humans and AI

Human-Centered Collaboration

Why are we always thinking about whether machines will replace human beings? This can never be possible. Machines need human beings to create or run them.

There is talk about artificial intelligence (AI) and whether it will replace human beings.

What is your opinion?

In what way can they replace human beings? They can collaborate with human beings, and they can help human beings, but they cannot replace them. Both have a role to play.

If we are talking about the work that machines can do and human beings cannot do, we can say the machines are only helping human beings as things can be done faster through them.

We used to calculate manually, and record-keeping took a long time. I remember when I did my PhD it was very difficult to calculate the data for the 400 companies in my sample.

Today, we can put the numbers down, and the machine will calculate quickly and give the result. This is a collaboration between human beings and machines, and we can achieve a lot.

I had to visit people personally to get data from them. I also sat in libraries for a long time, but today everything is found on the internet. The latest that is added is artificial intelligence to help people and not become a part of them.

How can AI write like a human being? It does not have consciousness. It is like a rubber ball. You have to move it the way you want to, but writers are becoming slaves to AI, taking copied material and using it everywhere.

This makes it difficult for honest writers who want to shine by writing their own human stories and contributions.

Consciousness of a human being / AI

According to psychologist LeDoux, there are four basic varieties of life on earth. These are biological, neurobiological, cognitive, and conscious. Most living things are in the biological realm.

He also states that only human beings and those with biological functions can have consciousness and not AI.

There has to be some element of consciousness to navigate and exercise control over new developments that have potential and freedom of expectations and actions.

To be human is to be able to reason and control one's behavior and actions. You learn to be a witness, observing what you experience and how you respond, and this comes from your sense of self.

Where does AI figure in all of this? LeDoux says only biological life can become conscious

Dennett, too, says that even if we artificially mimic biological attributes, the result will not endow the machine with intention or an agency with beliefs and desires. AI is not an intentional system that can make willful choices.

To understand the potential indicators of consciousness in AI, an interdisciplinary approach is vital, so that all aspects of life and evolution are covered. Though some life forms other than humans are observed to have a certain degree of consciousness, it is doubtful that this is a possibility in AI. That's what many scientists have concluded—but so far, the jury is still out.

The relevance of human beings and artificial intelligence (AI) is a complex and evolving topic that encompasses various dimensions, including technological, societal, ethical, and philosophical aspects.

Here are some key points regarding the relevance of both:

Complementary capabilities: Human beings have unique cognitive abilities. They are creative, they have emotional intelligence, and they have a high degree of intuition. AI does not have these capabilities.

AI systems are mechanical as they help with tasks that require data processing and automation.

This brings about the synergy between humans and AI, and these are complementary strengths.

Technology development: AI technology has been very useful in various sectors such as healthcare, finance, manufacturing, and transportation. They are useful in faster processing, greater efficiency, accuracy, and decision-making.

Ethical considerations: AI has created many discussions and ethical questions concerning privacy, security, bias, and accountability. These are questions that have to be discussed and developed, and we have no answers yet. We hope human beings will consider and be rational about these issues.

What are the takeaways?

1. It is expected that people may lose their jobs because AI will work faster and need fewer people. However, technicians, engineers, and technical hands will always be required to run these machines, so it is possible that new job opportunities may come up, particularly in AI research and development.

2. There will be collaboration between AI and human beings. They will not be competitors. When Google was first introduced. It brought in a lot of information through the network and you can sit at home and learn many skills. People were not keen to use the facility, but now they find it useful and important. It should be used as a tool and not as the main function of performance.

3. AI will become a super Google to give information on healthcare, education, and resources. It is already being used for surgeries and procedures in healthcare for heart, cancer, and other ailments. So its contribution cannot be undermined.

4. The human mind will always be superior and if there is interdisciplinary collaboration and proper governance frameworks it will not have very high risk to humanity.

To wrap up

The relevance of human beings and AI will be collaborative as technology progress will continue. Solutions will come out over technological progress, ethical considerations, societal impacts, and collaborative work.

There has to be a balance between AI and human work being carried out. There are challenges but collective action and discussions will make it possible to make it collaborative and less risky.

Reference

1 Joseph LeDoux, Ph.D.(2023), Our Four Realms of Existence: The Biological Realm, Every living thing that has ever existed has existed biologically, Psychology Today, https://www.psychologytoday.com/us/blog/i-got-a-mind-to-tell-you/202310/our-four-realms-of-existence-the-biological-realm

Lisa Precious

LISA PRECIOUS IS A spiritual guide, coach, and entrepreneur who has dedicated her life to supporting people in their spiritual journey. Lisa provides the tools to help people dissolve old beliefs and systems that no longer serve them, helping them realize who they are.

Lisa's passion for supporting people comes from her experiences of overcoming trauma in a dysfunctional family. Her healing journey led her to discover her purpose which is to help people on their spiritual journey to attain their highest growth potential.

Lisa's spiritual gifts allow her to provide her clients with unmatched guidance, unravelling their life, pinpointing their obstacles, and guiding them to their realizations. Her ability to provide information nobody else could have known often astounds her clients.

Lisa's greatest challenge was coming to terms with and understanding the abuse cycle, but this challenge ultimately led her to

God and higher consciousness. Lisa believes every life experience is an opportunity for growth and that we must take full responsibility for our lives to achieve success.

Smiley Blue is Lisa's way of painting more smiles in the world. The brand's vision is to bring happiness to people and align them with nature's principles in a fun, refreshing, exciting, and innovative way.

For Lisa, the world we see today is only a reflection of our conscious thoughts, and stepping back into the magnificent human beings we are is the key to achieving peace in the world.

Lisa Precious Email- smileybluecoaching@gmail.com

AI's Inorganic Surge and the Vital Connection of Human Creativity

Paving the way for an organic and connected reality

AI and creative writing

For writers, where does artificial intelligence (AI) fit in? Creative writing is organic; it's the divine creation, expressing one's thoughts. AI has no connection to the divine that we are and has no heart to express its emotions.

To craft this piece, I needed to take some time to be calm, gather my thoughts, and picture the world of AI, comparing this to how I envision the world of human intelligence (HI).

I give a little smile to myself as I recognize that AI can't meditate before it generates its response, whereas meditation is something that I always do prior to writing; I pray for inspiration and knowledge.

AI makes me think of the poor Tin Man from The Wizard of Oz, who wants a heart because he wants to feel and experience the emotions of a human being.

You see, it takes a heart to write a heartfelt message. And, when we write from this place, it connects us with other fellow human beings who resonate with our hearts and minds. We have something unique within each of us, and no artificial robot can ever replace what it is to be a human.

Through my writing alone, I have connected with incredible people who have lovingly shared and supported my journey.

The dichotomy between AI and HI

WHEN I THINK DEEPLY about AI, several words come to mind — artificial, inorganic, plastic, fake, dangerous, impersonal, disconnected, anti-human. By comparison, when I think about HI, words like creation, organic, blossoming, growth, nature, truth, heartfelt, honesty, integrity, love, and earth come to mind.

AI is currently and rightfully a hot topic, and we are beginning to see that people with foresight have connected the dots and sensed the potential dangers ahead.

We need a boundary line, and perhaps there lies the heart (there goes that word again) of the problem. There isn't a boundary, and people already feel uneasy and powerless to stop the AI surge ahead of us.

It's up to us to decide

HUMANITY HAS ALREADY accepted AI into everyday life; we can no longer function without being attached to our mobile tracking devices. Have you ever searched your bag, pockets, and house and felt the sheer panic of losing your phone?

Last year, my husband and I visited a restaurant in our hotel one evening. We were handed a QR code on a plastic square to scan the menu. Wanting no distractions from a phone and some precious time together, I purposely left my device in the hotel room.

I asked for a paper menu, and let's face it, we all still want to open a paper menu, don't we? It's part of the surprise and joy of eating out. Worried I wasn't happy, the waiter promptly went to print me one out. I guess I was making a statement that not all of us depend on our phones all the time.

I believe it doesn't take everyone to create change in the world. It is a positive sign that people are beginning to sense discomfort with the AI mission creep. Love and human intelligence have a natural way of pulling through all adversity.

The Internet's global impact

When the internet came online for the public, how exciting was it to receive an email or visit an online store? The internet has proven to be an incredible tool for making the world a smaller place, instantly connecting and aligning us with people in the world. Meetings are hosted from all corners of the globe—we don't even have to leave home to attend.As with everything, there is a dark side. The web is used to traffic children, drugs, and weapons, as well as opening up a can of worms for child abuse and online harm.

AI, THE NEXT GLOBAL takeover

AI may go the same way. It all depends on the level of consciousness behind the technology.

I believe many will sleepwalk themselves into an alternative metaverse reality to escape the one in which they barely have any meaningful existence. Although sad, this does not dishearten me.

On a more positive note, many people already envision a more organic, connected, and unified future.

You and I are the pioneers who put our intentions towards creativity and co-creating an organic, connected reality.

Warren Brown

WARREN BROWN HAS BEEN a self-published author with several fiction and non-fiction books on Amazon KDP, Smashwords, and Draft2Digital publishing platforms for over a decade. Warren enjoys writing science-fiction, thrillers, and adventures as well as poetry, stories, and articles.

Warren Brown is published Author, Publishing Consultant, Poet, Copywriter, Life Coach, and Internet Marketer. Warren is a British author of Anglo-Indian descent and lives in London with his wife.

Warren is working on a few novels, with several short stories and novel plots on the back burner. Warren Brown has published books on Internet Marketing, short stories, poetry, Life Coaching, cookery, e-commerce, and the Anglo-Indian community.

Warren has been a self-published author with several fiction and non-fiction books on multiple publishing platforms for over a decade. He enjoys writing science fiction, thrillers, adventures as well as poetry, and articles on Life Coaching.

As a result of his range of interests, he likes writing on a large variety of topics in several niches. This is good, as I attract several readers from different niches, who like to read his work. As an author, he knows that he is a work in progress and still needs to learn his craft and hopefully, one day write and publish a Bestseller.

Warren has a Bachelor of Arts degree with Honours in English and a Master of Science in Environment and Ecology. Warren has completed several diploma courses in Life Coaching, Social Work with Children and Families, Copywriting (American Writers and Artists Inc.), Library Science, how to be an Effective Administrator, Fundraising, and Entrepreneurship. Warren is a qualified Life Coach and Hypnotherapist.

Watching movies and serials is one of Warren's great hobbies besides reading and writing. A few of Warren's favorite movies and serials are any Tarzan movies, Zorro, the Lone Ranger, "Back to the Future", "Star Wars" and "Elementary", "Sherlock", "The Mentalist", "Criminals Minds", "The Black List" and "Lie to Me". Warren loves drawing and reading comics too. He also enjoys listening to music and dancing.

Warren believes in Miracles and the Power of the Individual to make a positive difference in the world today.

Does AI Art Look Like Masterpieces of Famous or Popular Artists?

At the beginning of this craze for AI art generation, several programs used the art of popular artists to train their art generators. It reached a point where the original art created by comic book artists was being reproduced by AI art generators.

It is now possible to create art in the *styles* of popular artists. However, it is not the same as the art produced by real, living, and breathing artists. There are so many art generators on the web today, and one seems to be better than the last one. A few of the AI. art generators that I use are Night Cafe and Leonardo.

I started by trying to create various AI compositions by simply writing prompts and asking the generator to create works of art for me. In most cases, the art generated was imperfect. I later learned that it was possible to request the AI art generator not to create imperfections in the art with the help of negative prompts, like "do not add wings, do not produce double heads, imperfect bodies, and fused fingers."

I know that the art I produce with the help of AI art generators for my writings and for the comic books that I create is not fantastic. The images produced do not resemble those of any great or popular artists. I have heard that the platforms take a few styles by several artists and then blend them, using artificial intelligence, to create recognizable images.

AI vs. HI Art—Comparisons

Many people enjoy creating and viewing AI art. However, it is always worth keeping in mind that the use of AI art needs to be monitored. We need to remember that there are human artists, and the art of humanity has endured for years and throughout human civilization.

In my opinion, AI-generated art is not perfect. Conceivably, it can but should never replace human art and artists. Art done by human beings is special as it helps them express their creativity and imagination. No matter how fantastic AI-generated art may appear to be, even when sold at high prices in auctions, it will never be able to replace human-created art.

AI-generated art, in my opinion, lacks the soul and the individuality of the artist. AI-created art does not express life, the experiences of the soul of the human heart, or the creative power of the human mind. Artificially generated art is a hotchpotch of ideas combined to form a somewhat coherent picture. However, keep in mind that AI can inspire an artist to create his or her fantastic works of art. I love AI art, as it inspires me to write stories and poems and to create ideas for comic books.

When an artist gets inspired, he or she proceeds to draw or paint a picture to express that creative idea with the necessary skills of sketching and painting. AI can analyse a vast amount of data to generate new and unique concepts that might inspire an artist to create masterpieces of human art for the world to appreciate and enjoy.

If I wanted to create a piece of art and told a human artist to draw and paint a picture of "a woman walking on the beach, towards the sunset," it would be done for me, but it would cost me, as the artist needs to survive. If I wanted a comic book artist to create the artwork for a comic based on one of my stories, I would need to pay the artist, and it would be pretty expensive for me. The artist will create every graphic, taking a lot of time and effort. The artist needs to be paid in full for all the work done and for their skills and expertise.

On the other hand, AI art is a lot cheaper, mostly free, and can create a variety of artwork, based on my prompt, "a woman walking on the beach, towards the sunset." I can have several variations of the artwork that I can use for as long as I want, and it is all owned by me though I cannot, at this time, register a copyright.

Almost all art generator websites give you the rights to the artwork you generate as your intellectual property, which you can use wherever and whenever you want, from book covers, posters, T-shirts, mugs, and calendars, and it is all free.

Is it also possible to incorporate AI art into the creative process? Yes, it can be done, and I do this regularly to illustrate my stories and my comic books.

The disadvantage of using AI art is that human artists may be unemployed. People may get lazy and stop creating their artwork. The skills of art, imagination, and creativity in humans will be lost. AI art lacks empathy and any form of human emotion or human experience.

Therefore, I can conclude that AI art could be used when needed for particular projects where rough images lacking human experience are required. Some human artists believe that AI art lacks the emotional depth and authenticity that come with human creativity.

When powerful art filled with human life experiences is needed, it is right to employ human artists. As a writer and an artist with human intelligence, I will always support human artists.

Annelise Lords

I AM ANNELISE LORDS and I love art and to create. I love to think, write, read, walk, cook, bake, and watch sunrises and sunsets. I listen with a third ear and use common sense to see and understand life, living, and humanity. Annelise has published multiple books adn her art can be found on many online platforms.

HI from the Heart—AI from Where?

HI writers write from the heart and have used innovative, creative ways of provoking and stimulating deep thoughts. I like using my brain; it's my CPU. It's also a tape recorder. I record the good and bad actions, choices, and decisions of everyone I communicate with and associate with. It's stored inside my brain, awaiting their bad or good action and intention. It's also a whiteboard. I write things on it too. I can read and understand emotions in HI writings.

HI writers write from the heart and have used innovative, creative ways of provoking and stimulating deep thoughts, forcing us to feel what the writers are feeling, along with understanding and the ability to heal through words. Sending our thoughts deep into areas of the brain, heart, and soul that nothing else can.

AI writers write about what someone tells them to. They lack the feeling and understanding to connect with writers and what they experience. Their emotions are empty because they come from a place where there are no feelings.

HI writers write from their experience or what they see happen to someone they love and know. They are connected to their emotions, experiences, and what life teaches them. Their power of words heals and helps—from the best part of humanity. The heart.

HI writers' instincts are alive, and many use them positively.

AI can't use what they don't have.

AI would have to be alive and live a life to understand life, living, pain, love, hatred, kindness, cruelty, forgiveness, understanding, honesty, peace, and all the other emotions or qualities that make humans what they are.

AI writers lack the ability to invoke thoughts or feelings. So, they have no real thought or feeling of what you have experienced. How can they motivate and uplift you if they have no idea or understanding of what you have been through?

AI can't write from the heart because they don't have a heart. They don't have a place of love, understanding, kindness, or feelings to write from. They lack the tools and experience that an innovative, imaginative heart, mind, and soul possess.

Sadly, there are humans with the behavior and actions of AI who live a life without feelings, love, kindness, imagination, or what it takes to be human.

Since humans are behind AI creations, we already know the kind of people we are dealing with. Many are creating themselves. We know humans. We already know what AI is capable of. Stop stressing and adding fear to your life. If machines are made to imitate us, then we know their intentions. AI has no heart. We already know the intentions of heartless humans. If anything, we should be prepared for their intentions because we already know them.

AI shows us the real side of many humans and how dangerous allowing them to control our lives will be.

AI isn't a competition for us. How can anyone sensible and sane use fake to compete with real? But since humanity strives for perfection, competition will always be there.

HI writers are in control, and many of us can identify who is whom. There shouldn't be competition between humans and machines because the machines are made by humans. Makes no sense. It's like creating your own enemy and competing against yourself. I don't see AI as a threat because it has no heart, imagination, or feeling. But I do.

Libby Shively McAvoy

Libby Shively McAvoy is a Personal Development and Relationship Coach specializing in Emotional Intelligence. Having survived both physical and emotional abuse, Libby believes strongly that increasing emotional intelligence has the ability to decrease school-age bullying as well as abuse in adult years and increase personal success overall in life.

She combines her life experience, coaching and 500hr yoga certifications for a successful career. Libby enjoys motivational speaking, leading wellness, meditation, & yoga retreats globally, writing, parenting, traveling, cooking, & seeking knowledge.

Her mission is to awaken, inspire, and empower others to stop living on autopilot and to start living the life they love.

Artificial Intelligence Cannot Replace Emotional Intelligence

Would you want your significant other to be a robot?

Artificial intelligence has its pluses and minuses.

I believe we need to look at artificial intelligence from all perspectives, just like anything else in life. Personally, it scares me, and I still prefer human and emotional intelligence. I understand that AI is gaining emotional awareness, which intimidates me. I don't want to communicate with a bot. This will likely be a great distance in the future if it does happen.

The plus side of AI

1. In the dating world, artificial intelligence sorts and pinpoints possible matches based on personal experiences and preferences. This saves a lot of time and the heartbreak of bad dates. Let's face it—that is a big perk. It is not that online dating is always a positive experience, but I have heard it has come a long way.
2. In the medical world, robotic instruments aid in surgical procedures. This has not yet replaced doctors, thankfully, in my humble opinion, but someday it might.
3. When bombs are detected, robots are used to diffuse them.

This saves the possibility of harming human lives.

I AM SURE THERE ARE many more great uses for artificial intelligence. McDonalds has begun implementing AI in some locations as a way of ensuring precision. Unfortunately, this limits human jobs. Is it worth the "quality" of service?

Robots and AI cannot ever replace the emotional intelligence that humans naturally possess. Do we want to trade speed and precision for quality and connection? Even people with low emotional intelligence can develop higher levels at any stage of life. Robots can never build empathy.

How do you feel about this issue? If your job were replaced by artificial intelligence, what would you do, and how would you feel?

If you walked into stores and there were no humans to help you, would you feel frustrated? I sure would. I know when I go into Home Depot, for example, I appreciate the older gentlemen who kindly direct me to what I need to find, which saves me time and effort.

Final thoughts

IF YOUR INTIMATE PARTNER was not romantic and you could program a new partner, would that be ideal? Maybe if you have been betrayed, you might think this would sound good at first. But think about it long term. It would get cold and old. A human gives you a run for your money. Their defiance and chase keep life exciting. You want some spice.

I think artificial intelligence will take over many skills, but if you have a career that thrives on emotional intelligence, like counseling, coaching, nursing, or anything similar, you will thrive. Maybe it is time to reassess. Protect yourself by boosting your emotional intelligence.

Gary Friedman

GARY L. FRIEDMAN IS a Photographer, Author, and Lecturer. Gary is a NASA veteran who has been monitoring the AI field for decades. You can find Gary through The Friedman Archives

Travel stock photography gallery at www.FriedmanArchives.com[1]. Gary is the Associate Editor for Cameracraft magazine

www.friedmanarchives.com/cameracraft[2]. Gary's best-selling e-books on Sony, Fujifilm, and OM-Digital cameras:

www.FriedmanArchives.com/ebooks[3].

1. http://www.friedmanarchives.com/
2. http://www.friedmanarchives.com/cameracraft
3. http://www.friedmanarchives.com/ebooks

Humans Will Need A Label

IT SEEMS THAT AI HAS exploded onto the scene (at least all the tech news outlets), some of them positive ("ChatGPT can find case law faster and easier than using conventional keyword searches") (oh wait, that's a lie!), but most of them negative ("Look at all of these factual errors it's confidently spitting out!!", or "This can be used to easily create malware!"). Then I read that some people have empathy for these things, and some have been using chatbots to write books with little to no effort and self-publish them on Amazon, with the promise of exponentially amplifying the amount of crap out there. As they proliferate, we'll need some humans to sort through what's factually correct to increase the value of its output. Back in my day, those people were called "editors".

It then occurred to me that there will soon be a need for certification - similar to what the farmers' associations came up with to let consumers know whether their crops were organic, or whether a food product contained preservatives. There will be a need for people who don't want to double-check every fact spit out by a chatbot, to know that what they're consuming has had some human quality control on it to weed out demonstrable falsehoods (Flat Earth? 5G towers cause COVID?), label rumors appropriately ("Climate Change is a hoax from China"), and to give proper historical context. Plus, it's been demonstrated that those tools that can allegedly detect if ChatGPT had been used to create something are about as reliable as the chatbot output they're trying to authenticate.

So while in the past I proposed a law firm that would sue the misbehaving AI models and whip them into shape, I now propose that all content created without the use of AI be voluntarily labeled as such. Of course, definitions would have to be worked out, just as it had with farming (there were many definitions of "organic" in the beginning, for example). And there will be shades of grey even for photographers - for example, should Photoshop (which has some AI tools built-in) count?

Taking this idea a step further, I recall how typewritten letters were once highly regarded when they first appeared, conveying an aura of importance and stature and those were the letters people opened first. Then when printed letters became the norm, handwritten letters suddenly stuck out as being novel and attention-worthy. And I think the same thing might happen in photography. Currently there's no image on the internet that hasn't been post-processed in some way. I wonder if in the near future scanned transparencies with no post-processing will somehow become more valued because they tell the "truth" more than images that have been manipulated to look more pleasing (which is usually synonymous with lying). Traditionalists can make their mark by being different - only producing straight-out-of-camera images!!! Getting it right in the camera like we used to back in the day!!! Same idea - you're certifying that the content was created by a human and not by a machine learning algorithm.

AI The Alarmists Are Worrying About The Wrong Thing

Ever since ChatGPT appeared, and the world has gone nuts, especially in the field of education where essay exams are an integral part of assessing understanding and articulateness. Enlightened educators have embraced it, insisting students use the tool, inform them that they are responsible for any factual errors that result, and that use of the tool must be disclosed. ChatGPT has also demonstrated that it can debug computer code better than the traditional tools. On the downside, the demand for real writers will go down and fluff (and disinformation, no doubt) on the internet will increase exponentially.

Any new technology introduces risks and benefits; AI is no different. And society will adjust, just like it has when the Scitex machine (and later Photoshop) eroded the credibility of the image. (Heck, society even adapted to the introduction of contraceptives and television, both of which completely upended the way we live. AI is just another in a long string of disruptive technologies.)

I say this as a prelude to this observation: all of the alarmists complaining about the new wave of AI and what it implies about creativity and ownership are completely ignoring the real AI threat, which started to appear about 10 years ago and is already ruining people's lives.

===

Computer scientists have been working on AI since the 1960's. It's taken many decades to get where we are today, and what we have today is pretty brain dead compared to the industry's ambitious goals:

to be able to have an intelligent conversation with an algorithm; to have the machine display characteristics of thought. Something that can pass the Turing test. There have been some significant developments; I remember back in the 1980's attending an AI conference where a professor was demonstrating a program that could read Romeo and Juliette and answer difficult conversational questions about the story. It was impressive, especially since it was written in Fortran (at a time when Lisp was the preferred language for such things).

But because AI had not lived up to the lofty promises, and the industry had to do something to bring in revenue, an offshoot of the field developed called "Expert Systems" - algorithms that could make decisions so humans don't have to. Really it was just machine learning. They were awful. I distinctly remember one of the instructional videos for a commercial product at the time: "Notice how the system made a mistake, just like a real expert would". That was the moment that the entire field of expert systems lost credibility in my mind.

Fast forward to today, and very little has changed. What people are now touting as "AI" is really machine learning, and it's just as flawed as the expert systems of the 1990's. Worse, bureaucrats who don't understand technology are going ga-ga over this new, shiny AI stuff and they are implementing it in irresponsible ways: approving or denying mortgage applications or university applications. Deciding about health benefits. Approving / denying credit cards by piecing together everything about your online presence and then judging your character worthiness for credit. Wrongly denying welfare recipients their benefits and then charging them for fraud. Screening out perfectly qualified people who apply for jobs online. Filter social workers' calls and then disproportionately flag disabled parents for child abuse. AI AS IT'S CURRENTLY DEPLOYED IS RUINING PEOPLE'S LIVES. Worse, unlike that demonstration I saw in the 80's, these current machine learning algorithms cannot explain how they arrived at their decisions. So companies blindly trust its output, and there is very little recourse for a person who has been wrongly denied a service or benefit due to these products. And the bureaucrats love it: "Look at all those expensive people we won't have to hire!"

But unlike a human decision maker, you can actually prove that these machine learning algorithms are biased. Take the code and run a bunch of sample data through it and you can demonstrate in front of a judge that the algorithm makes skewed and potentially unfair decisions.

So what's my next business idea? Start a law firm that specializes in suing so-called "AI" companies that are wrongly denying people access to essential resources or services. Provide a modicum of accountability for an industry that lacks it, and restore a semblance of fairness to those people who play by the rules.

This is the latest of many examples where the engineers invent something cool (without adequate consideration of the potential negative consequences), and the bureaucrats blissfully mis-apply it as a cool cost-saving measure. And we all pay the price. Right about now, this is where the lawyers step in and save civilization from irresponsible deployment of an immature technology.

Once my proposed solution is deployed, in about 10 years all of these AI biases will be exposed and repaired, resulting in automated decisions that are actually fairer than what a human would do.

DON'T SAY I DIDN'T warn you. Check out this article: Denied by AI: How Medicare Advantage plans use algorithms to cut off care for seniors in need. https://tinyurl.com/4vwh4swb

Dan Pelland

BEHIND EVERY GREAT content platform lies a technical genius, and for many websites, that's Dan Pelland. As a skilled programmer and web developer, he has provided seamless and enjoyable user experiences. His expertise in web design and development allows him to create visually stunning and user-friendly web presences

A professional writer, with a background in photography and graphic design, Dan creates both content and visual elements. His years of experience have established his artistic flair, content development skills, and technical know-how. For two years, Dan has studied and mastered AI platforms for images and text-to-voice technology.

Ethical Use of OpenAI's ChatGPT

What will we do with the bucket of worms that is AI?

I'm an engineer. My wife, Maryan Pelland, is a writer. I'm super fascinated and excited by tech stuff, especially artificial intelligence. Maryan, not so much.

Recently, I found out just how crazy-amazing, and some would say scary, ChatGPT4 is. By combining chat with text-to-speech (both OpenAI products), I found out that I could produce really good material, in the form of spoken words, perfect for, let's say, a podcast. I got a great deal of satisfaction from making and then listening to imaginary speakers, with voices as rich as any professional actor, recite the passages I had curated.

Being the dumbass that I am (yeah, engineers can be dumbasses too), I approached Maryan like an eight-year-old with a new model airplane, to show her what I had made. I didn't expect the response I got. Maybe I should have, though.

As a writer, her allegiance is to her community of professionals and freelancers struggling to eke out a few bucks for the time they spend crafting a well-written essay or article. Okay, I get it. Also, note that my next sentence does not begin with the word BUT.

Writing is hard. Chat is easy; I think it's probably too easy, if I'm being honest. But if nothing else, AI is opening a bucket of worms that we're all going to have to deal with, one way or another.

The method I use creates audio speech files. They are MP3's like the ones you can download and playback through your laptop or smartphone. They sound great, and are very lifelike. My voice character's computer name is "Onyx." It's a stock voice profile from Open AI that comes with their TTS (text to speech) application programming interface (API).

I wrote a simple Python script to generate the MP3 files. Each paragraph of text becomes a single file. I place the files into a timeline in Audacity[1] and compose the final product. So far, so good, right? If I use this new technology to generate speech from my own original material, it's all good.

The problem is that some folks would get bent if I used words generated by the chatbot instead of my own. It is understood that chat uses words and phrases—and, some believe, entire works of art—to generate its output. The extent to which original art becomes a product of the chatbot, as I understand it, isn't known, even by the people who created the AI platforms.

Consider this. If I asked chat to read a technical academic article that people like me would have a hard time understanding and translate the article's content into an interesting essay appropriate for a 10th-grade reader, would that be plagiarism? As much as I'd like to believe it would not, I have to respect the opinions of others who disagree.

So, the issue now becomes: Is there any way I can leverage AI to produce media that has meaningful benefits for everyone, not just me, and still respects the intellectual property of the millions of authors, artists, researchers, scientists, and philosophers whose hard work got digitized, downloaded, and blended into large language models—the soup of AI's brand of human intelligence?

What is the current status of rules and regulations concerning the use of AI? The US Copyright Office has asked for opinions from interested parties and, as of the date of this article, filed a Notice of Inquiry, also known as an N-O-I, in the Federal Register. The NOI

1. https://www.nch.com.au/index.html

is a preliminary step toward advising Congress on rule-making and regulations regarding the ethical use of AI.

Until regulations tell me otherwise, I've decided to keep making my hobby podcasts. If I publish one or two, I'll be sure to attribute any original material I use. I will post a notice that the content was created with the help of AI, and I will research the topics using reliable sources to make sure the facts are facts and not misrepresentations or mistakes.

For a while, maybe a long while, humans may have to really focus on ways to use AI without stepping on the toes and rights of other humans. We will need to be careful of how we choose to use these tools.

Use AI Wisely and You Might Create Enormous Benefits for Humankind

Content creation is a big industry with a bright future. Like a Valentine's Day gift, on February 14, 2005, YouTube was born and instantly became the internet's most used platform for content creators. A low threshold of entry made YouTube suddenly and wildly popular. Even solo practitioners could participate with only a small investment.

For example, a thirteen-year-old with a cell phone, a fair amount of ambition, and some human intelligence can create a YouTube video. Life is good in the YouTube lane. Creators are making significant money without forking out lots of cash.

Then it gets even better

On November 30, 2022, ChatGPT was released to the public. Artificial intelligence, which, for years, we believed was on the same track as flying cars, suddenly shifted from science fiction to reality. Within months, Google, Adobe, and a few other companies were scrambling to leverage the power of artificial intelligence.

They adapted their specialized tools—Photoshop and Illustrator for graphics, Microsoft Word or GoogleDocs for text, and a number of options for speech, music, and sound effects. Now, these tools connect artificial and human intelligence.

AI tools have reshaped the world for creators.

My personal journey

As a creator, I'm always looking for opportunities in this new space, and I thought my background in programming gave me an advantage.

But technology is moving so fast that I can no longer rely on my past experience to guide me with current technology. Instead, I use YouTube to stay up-to-date. Ambitious creators share tutorials, information about new tools, and reviews—kind of like a "University of YouTube." I find these invaluable.

As soon as ChatGPT appeared, I jumped on the AI bandwagon. I hit all the AI tech giant websites and found that access was easy and the cost was low. I opened developer accounts at OpenAI, Google, Amazon, Microsoft, and a few others.

These accounts connected me with everything I wanted to know about AI. I've played and experimented to my heart's content. As I'm writing this, ChatGPT is at version four, Midjourney is at five, ElevenLabs is becoming frighteningly capable, and I'm yearning to do something useful with the AI insight I've gained. Here's that insight:

(1) Chatbots are useful, but not for writing, as some people had hoped. The output is easily recognizable by its overuse of phrasing and repetitive vocabulary. Many people, especially those who write for a living, consider AI writing unethical, and I don't disagree. In my opinion, a better use case for a chatbot is research, but even in that respect, caution is advised. The bots return mostly accurate information, but we must employ the Russian proverb, "Trust but verify." The bots output generally readable information without advertisements, so far at least, and sometimes they even include useful citations.

(2) Some bots, ChatGPT-4 in particular, write excellent programming code. But knowing what to do with the code can be a bump in the road unless you have coding experience. On the upside, ChatGPT-4 plus a few good YouTube tutorials can be a great way to learn programming. Here's a hint: Start with Python.

(3) Midjourney is my favorite AI "artist" because it's easy to use, inexpensive, and produces consistent output that gets better with every

new release. I have used it to make illustrations for a few of the articles I've written on Medium.com.

More often, I use it to make wall art for our home. It may be useful for commercial artists (I'm not one) to some extent, especially now that Midjourney's programmers have fine tuned its ability to produce text that makes sense within an illustration.

There's another area of AI that I think is most interesting.

AI creates human voices

Text-to-speech (TTS) is a shining example of how artificial intelligence can have a positive impact on humanity's future. Take a paragraph of text, run it through a TTS app, and you will be amazed at how like human speech the output sounds. Recent developments in the quality of speech processing software have created a great opportunity for solo content creators and another way to make new and useful contributions to the tapestry of the internet.

We're not all proficient readers. Many people, myself included, have forms of dyslexia that make it hard to read or to comprehend what we have read. I really enjoy someone reading to me while I listen with my eyes closed. I'm pretty sure others do, too. The success of Amazon's Audible and other audiobook platforms proves that point.

On another note, according to the World Health Organization, over a billion people worldwide live with vision impairment. Consider that 70% of all internet content is consumed on mobile devices (cell phones). Small screens and tiny text make reading difficult, even for those with 20-20 vision.

I have a feeling there is still a lot of literary art and written information out there that could be made accessible to a wider, much more inclusive audience through high-quality spoken-word transcription.

These accessibility issues are especially important in the context of education. Many young students struggle with reading in school.

Personalized, adaptive learning experiences based on TTS generated content could help students of all abilities.

Anyone reading this essay is aware of the era of television and the internet, though these are very recent inventions. Given that the spoken word has been the predominant currency of communication for well over 99% of human existence, it's clear that our voices and the voices of our predecessors are of great value. It would be a wonderful undertaking to resurrect and preserve texts and stories from a multitude of cultures by translating them and transcribing them into high-quality human speech.

We see the value in radio broadcasts and in podcasts, but as speech synthesis improves, we're also seeing text-first platforms providing audio transcriptions of their content. These include popular magazines and major newspapers. On Medium, for instance, it's easy to click on the *listen* icon under every title and listen to a fairly good screen-reader narration.

A window in the cloud

THERE IS AN OPPORTUNITY to create high-quality audio content from text with AI. The simple screen-readers that have been around for a long time don't always generate the quality a listener would expect. However, the most recent versions of Eleven Labs, OpenAI's Text to Speech API, and the Google Cloud Text to Speech API can convert text into remarkably natural sounding speech—in multiple languages, no less.

Eleven Labs is the easiest. Create a free account, and you can transcribe 10,000 characters per month. That's enough to get a feel for the process and evaluate the quality of the voices. Other monthly options for Eleven Labs include $5 for 30,000 characters, or $22 for 100,000 characters. Since I began using Eleven Labs in 2021, I've noticed steady improvements in the platform's features and the quality of the voices.

The OpenAI and Google TTS engines, called *application programming interfaces* (API's), require a degree of programming skill. It took me about half a day to implement the OpenAI version. I used the Microsoft VSCode editor and the example code that OpenAI provides on their website. If you're interested, look up one of the many tutorials on YouTube that explain the details of implementing these excellent TTS apps.

The last word

Some people's lives will benefit from having enhanced access to more spoken language than is currently available. Just as the internet democratized writing in general, we are realizing how AI can make more ideas, information, entertainment, and literary art available to a wider audience.

These technologies are sure to change. Some will improve our lives—others not so much. The spoken word is the hallmark of humanity, predating even the rise of civilization. We need to be cautious when adopting AI, but it's clear that there are excellent opportunities for prudent content creators to leverage AI to the benefit of mankind.

Janin Lyndovsky

Janin Lyndovsky has a successful career in the IT field. She has been in this field for well over 25 years, holding various positions (currently as a domain architect) and often working with the most modern technologies, including Blockchain, Machine Learning and Artificial Intelligence. However, she doesn't like to be defined through the prism of her professional life. She is passionate about people, and her dream is to inspire others to believe in themselves and follow their dreams.

Janin was born in communist Poland, where she learned at a very young age that happiness doesn't depend on what we have but on how grateful we are for what we have. Though her family didn't have much material wealth, they were very happy. Unfortunately, her life changed when she attended high school. At the same time, her beloved grandfather died, and she felt lost and lonely. At school, she wasn't accepted, often bullied, her parents faced financial hardship, and she went through a series of events that eventually left her with PTSD.

She didn't want to have the life of a victim, and decided to take her life into her own hands and change it for the better, firmly holding on to the words of her grandpa - "You can be whoever you want to be in life. Your life depends only on you".

At the age of 23, Janin went to Germany as an Au Pair. In one year, she completed three years of German language study and decided to remain in Germany and study there at one of the best technical universities in Europe. She studied Business Mathematics, with economics and computer science as minors. She was exposed to discrimination, struggled financially, and twice looked death in the eyes when she experienced NDE (once in sickness and once in accident). However, her determination paid off, and in 2005, she graduated with a Master's degree, which she called "the ticket to freedom" (the degree was recognised worldwide) and started a career in actuarial mathematics.

However, staying in Germany wasn't her dream, so in 2006, she left for Australia. She arrived on the driest continent on earth with a tourist visa and a "no further stay" condition in her passport. From the moment she laid her eyes on that country, she fell in love with it and knew she would make it her home. The first few years were very tough; she experienced homelessness and a lot of hardship. Nonetheless, it all paid off.

Now, she is an Australian by choice. She lives on a farm she loves, surrounded by nature and her beloved pets. She has a career she enjoys and is living her impossible childhood dream and having a happy and fulfilling life.

Her goal is to share her stories to show others that her grandpa was right: our life depends only and solely on us because it doesn't depend on what happens to us but on how we react to whatever happens to us. Janin can find a silver lining in the most hopeless situation and wants to inspire others to look at the bright side of every situation.

Her two favourite mottoes are "If you can dream it, you can do it!" and "Be You! Be Yourself! Believe in Yourself because you are special. There is only one of you!"

Artificial Intelligence—Curse or Blessing?

Artificial intelligence (AI) is a hot topic. Almost everyone talks about it and, in one way or another, uses it, sometimes even unknowingly. Some people, especially technology lovers, adore it and see it as our future—the best invention in human history. At the same time, others perceive it as a danger to our world and the end of humanity as we know it.

I have worked in IT for over two decades, often with the most modern technologies. There was a time when I worked on autonomous vehicles, and my preferred subject was aircraft. I have some knowledge about AI and ML (machine learning), and I find it useful in many areas of my profession.

On the other hand, I'm passionate about psychology, human behaviors and interactions, relationships, and mental health. I watch people and ponder their behavior in various situations without judging them.

What I have observed regarding people's opinions about AI, especially the extreme ones, is that often they are based on a lack of understanding of what AI actually is, how it works, and, in some cases, its complexity in incorporating it in our everyday lives.

An example of technology enthusiasts

JUST A FEW WEEKS AGO, I had a chat with an older gentleman, passionate about technology, who bought the newest model of Tesla with the "self-driving option." He expects that in a few months (with the next upgrade), his vehicle will be fully autonomous, and there won't be a need for a driver anymore. There was no point in trying to explain that, as the vehicles themselves are pretty much autonomous, we are a few years away from having fully automated cars on our roads.

As the technology is there to "make the vehicle drive without a driver," we face many issues on how to introduce the vehicles into our real world. We have to take into account weather, road, and traffic conditions. What will happen when a number of autonomous cars drive on the same road?

How would it affect their lidar signals? What about all the laws, state or federal laws, or accident liability? Not to mention that we still have plenty of legacy vehicles with human drivers and pedestrians on our roads. What if someone unexpectedly steps on the road? And that is where human intelligence plays a role. There is plenty of non-verbal communication between drivers and pedestrians, and that process can instinctively save lives.

Artificial intelligence is nothing but a number of algorithms analyzing data. The algorithms are mainly designed by humans, though AI has started creating some algorithms too. That's where AI vs. HI plays a role.

So yes, we have great technology supporting autonomous vehicles, but we are a few years away from seeing fully self-driving cars on our roads.

An example of technology skeptics

I CAME ACROSS AN ARTICLE saying we shouldn't use ChatGPT because "it is racist,discriminatory, and dangerous for our society."

That's like saying, "Do not use knives because knives are killers." Everyone knows that a knife is just a tool, and depending on how it is used, it can kill when used by a killer or save lives when used in the form of a scalpel by a doctor. There is a full palette of tasks we perform in everyday life that require the use of a knife, starting with using it in our kitchen to prepare food, utilising it as a tool in the garage, or creating art.

The same is true of ChatGPT. It's a tool, and whether it supports humanity or works against us depends only on us. We are the ones who put the input parameters into the system, and based on our input, ChatGPT gives us the answer.

We have to keep in mind that ChatGPT uses algorithms that, in a very short time, process tons of information floating on the Internet and provide answers based on this. There is a lot of rubbish in the cloud, so it is our responsibility to evaluate the response we get, and if we aren't convinced about its correctness, search for better answers.

This tool should serve to support us in gaining access to more information and making better decisions. However, to use it in our favor, we must use our human intelligence to evaluate how to use the tool to make it work in our favor and not against us.

The importance of our human intelligence

WHEN WE USE ARTIFICIAL intelligence, we must use human intelligence to verify the information AI provides us. I don't think we should have a competition or a fight between artificial intelligence and human intelligence. We should make these two work together in our favor. AI can support us humans in developing better medical and educational systems, better environments, and better communities.

I believe one of humanity's biggest problems is seeing everything as black and white, good or bad, us vs. them. It would be so much better if we united different aspects of life and took out of it what benefits us as a community and as a human race.

Yes, of course, there are risks that some individuals can misuse AI for their personal gains, power, and money. We can use our human intelligence and AI to protect ourselves from possible harm. Being scared of new technologies, hiding from them, or denying their existence wouldn't be a smart choice.

We have to learn how to embrace technology. Our ancestors were afraid of fires, but the human race advanced from the moment we learned to embrace fire and use it to our benefit.

What significant progress has humanity made since we discovered tools and ways of farming, not to mention the Industrial Revolution? Cars can kill us, but they are convenient to move from one place to another. Knives can kill us, yet they are handy in preparing food. AI could potentially kill and destroy us, but it's our choice to embrace it in a way that supports us in a better and happier life.

Will AI Eradicate Us as an Intelligent Species?

Artificial intelligence can be found in any area of our lives, from education to healthcare to automotive to entertainment, and even agriculture and legal uses of this technology. The goal is to improve the quality of life and support us as humans in having a healthier, more comfortable, and happier life.

But does AI support our lives, or does it reduce the need to exercise our brain/mind, and as a result, our skills in the areas of analytical, creative, critical, or any type of thinking become more and more limited?

AI gives us quick and easy access to information. Simplifies daily tasks like shopping, cooking, and many other basic chores—most households have smart devices. Our phone "thinks for us." Whatever we need to remember, we can set an alarm for. We don't need to remember the date of our loved ones' birthdays, think about what gifts to buy, or write on their birthday cards because the phone does it for us. ChatGPT will write the wishes and suggest gift ideas. At some point, we may barely know our loved ones.

Travel is easy, as our cars "think" for us, and the phone solves the problem of finding our way in unknown cities when we go for a walk.

Entertainment is at the press of a button— if we want to watch something or play a game, it's there at any time. We don't need to wait a week or two to see the next episode of our favorite series. An app will even tell us what we should watch or what is recommended for us. There are apps for whatever we want to do, telling us *how to live our lives*.

Healthcare is improving drastically, and diagnoses are becoming more accurate at earlier stages. As a result, chances of recovering from serious illnesses are much better, and people live longer. Yet, at the same time, mental health is deteriorating. More and more people suffer from depression or other mental health conditions, and the number of suicides is rising.

Is there a correlation between AI overtaking our lives and mental health? Is AI helping us become wiser and improve our lives, or does it make us less resilient and dumber?

Education

AI CAN BE VERY USEFUL in education to create adaptive learning platforms and personalized learning plans.

However, what about an average school child? Everything they need to complete their assignments can easily be found online. Many kids do not even have the skills to evaluate whether the given information is correct. They blindly believe what they find on Google or what ChatGPT spits out (which can be misleading as it is the result of imperfect algorithms scanning through limited information floating on the Internet). Many reliable sources do not allow ChatGPT to scan through their papers. Yes, if the information is for a school assignment, the teachers will correct it, but outside of school, the kids just trust the Internet. And this is fraught with danger.

We have great tools that can support students in learning, but at the same time, these tools can be their biggest enemies. Let's take a simple tool like Grammarly. It's a terrific tool for correcting spelling and grammatical errors or learning new vocabulary. But depending on how we use it, it can lead to a reduction in learning. We don't learn anything when we run the tool through our text and unquestioningly accept all changes. We would need to analyze every mistake to understand why it was incorrect, try to remember it, and memorize new vocabulary. If we don't, we won't be able to speak the language properly.

The fact is that the average person's vocabulary is probably becoming more and more limited, and most of us struggle to express our feelings and emotions. We can't clearly present our perception of a given situation. Sometimes, I wonder if our aim is to get back to cavemen times and express our emotions through emojis —-thumb up or down, feeling happy, sad, or angry. That's it. The lack of the ability to express ourselves may negatively impact our mental health.

Many educational tools can be supportive in our learning process if used in the right way. Therefore, it is vital that kids learn about the tools they use, how they work, and the best way to use them. Blindly believing the information we see on the Internet won't lead to development and growth.

Loss of authenticity

A BIG PART OF OUR LIVES happens online. What we see in the virtual world usually seems perfect. Everyone seems always cheerful and happy, smiling with immaculate appearances. These individuals have ideal body shapes and looks. They appear to have no problems.

While we scroll through the "perfect world," we don't realize that what we see isn't often real. Stories are written by ChatGPT (or should I say "content is generated by AI"; how should we even know if the events happened?) Images are designed by AI, and photos are edited to the point that the shade of reality is removed.

We start doubting ourselves, our looks, feelings, and thoughts. The "rest of the world" is perfect; there is something wrong with us; our lives are dull and boring. We aren't "good enough."

At this point, not only does our brain not get enough exercise in analytical and creative thinking, but we may be pushing ourselves into depression.

Social media and socializing

THESE DAYS, WE MAINLY socialize through social media. Many spend hours chatting with people they have never met while not having time for real-life friends. They do not have time to get to know the people living closest to them, try to understand them, and build proper relationships.

There is nothing wrong with interacting with people from all over the world; this can be beneficial, too, as long as we have real friends.

Romance scams are booming. Why? Because people miss connections and genuine, real-life friendships. Many of us miss love, affection, understanding, and compassion—things that make us humans. Some scams begin with AI - ChatGPT creating the best romantic answers to take advantage of the emotional emptiness the victims feel.

We are overwhelmed by the virtual world. We don't know what is real and what is fiction. We don't know if the images we see are real or AI-generated. Do we read authentic stories, or is it all machine-generated reality? We do not know whom to trust and whom to follow. We try to fit in, but we are losing our authenticity and identity. In the end, we do not even know who we are. That's a lot for our mental capacity to process.

Conclusion

WHAT I MENTIONED IN this article is the tip of the iceberg. AI may negatively affect our intellectual ability and mental health. The risk is real and seems to be growing from day to day.

Still, there is a lot of good AI can bring into our lives, too. Through AI, the world is becoming our oyster—we can communicate all across the globe, learn about any topic, visit faraway places without leaving our living room, or work in a dream job on the other end of the world while residing in a place we cherish.

AI may give us endless opportunities. However, we will only be able to benefit from them if we keep training and improving our human intelligence. If we neglect it, allow AI to do everything for us, and stop training our minds and exercising our brains, AI may overtake and destroy us.

A few individuals will control AI, but I doubt they will have the best intentions at heart. As we know, hackers and scammers don't have the best intentions and already often adversely influence our lives.

Gabriela Trofin-Tatár

GABRIELA TROFIN-TATÁR is an economist by profession and a blogger on Medium and Substack. With a passion for all things tech, she has been studying programming and new AI technologies as part of a career break during her maternity leave.

She has worked in a corporate organization as a leader in the operations department, always connecting people in various departments with B2B customers.

She likes to connect with people worldwide through her writing and projects, and she is interested in coaching and training others. She takes a particular interest in reading what other writers have expressed and is a continuous learner.

She has been part of the GE Women's Network, AIESEC alumni, Google Developers, a book blogger and book reviewer, and a content creator.

She is presently looking to enroll back in full-time work after her career break, eager to connect, share her knowledge, and continue to develop her skills in the knowledge management industry.

On her blogs, she shares her life as a mother of three, personal development, and travel experiences.

Topics about parenting, womanhood, travel, and technology interest her a lot. She also writes fiction and poetry. She is the owner and editor of the Simple Story Seekers publication.

She is passionate about reading, learning foreign languages (including programming languages), traveling and writing about travel, and hiking. She practices yoga and enjoys the health benefits of long nature walks.

She has a unique style of taking one thing at a time while always having plans in the queue for new adventures and learning opportunities. Always on the move, yet loving sleep and a good art exhibition occasionally.

Each day is a brand-new adventure for her. Her motto is "Believing in yourself is the best secret to success.".

Email: simplestoryseekers@gmail.com

Creativity and Originality in the Context of AI vs. HI

"According to Merriam-Webster[1], creativity is "the ability to create," with the verb "create" being a multi-dimensional term that implies the actions and behaviors that lead to the birth of something new."

Will we still be able to tell the difference ten years from now between AI and HI writing?

For the next ten years, the five big predictions in the context of AI development are focused on scientific changes and also developments at governmental and healthcare levels.

Forbes [2]doesn't mention anything about AI taking over HI. It's all about machine learning in science, big data for faster discoveries, global partnerships for AI advancements, the metaverse or cryptocurrencies, climate change with AI predictions, and personalised healthcare.

There is talk about AI giving humans a competitive edge in content creation in marketing, according to an article in [3]*Forbes*[4].

In their New Year predictions, Buffer[5].com said:

"Overall, while AI tools have been proven to provide efficiency and consistency, they also brought to light the need for human oversight to

1. *https://www.merriam-webster.com/dictionary/creativity*
2. *https://www.forbes.com/sites/forbesbusinesscouncil/2022/05/05/the-future-of-ai-5-things-to-expect-in-the-next-10-years/*
3. https://www.forbes.com/sites/forbescommunicationscouncil/2023/12/22/artificial-intelligence-and-the-future-of-content-marketing/
4. *https://www.forbes.com/sites/forbescommunicationscouncil/2023/12/22/artificial-intelligence-and-the-future-of-content-marketing/*
5. https://buffer.com/resources/2023-social-media-predictions-check-in/

maintain creativity, authenticity, and ethical standards in content creation. The year taught us a crucial lesson: the future of content creation lies in the synergy between AI and the irreplaceable human mind."

But what about creative writing?

When we think, however, of content creation for writers, the creativity and originality topic is not covered per se.

Either writers are busy using AI and not thinking about the consequences for the younger generations, or they are busy writing their original pieces and "battling" the generated content users.

"It's important to note that AI software does not create anything. It generates a regurgitation of what it's fed," the *Writers Guild of America*[6] has claimed[7].

There is already a faint line between AI content and HI content, but the difference lies exactly in what makes HI writing irreplaceable in the long run. And that is emotion expressed through words in a unique way, almost like an imprint, characteristic of each person who can express their inner thoughts through the written word.

Human creators are authentic

WHILE AI HAS MADE SIGNIFICANT strides in generating content, human creativity and originality still stand out. It will be forever unique, in my opinion, unless people suddenly stop writing original HI works and AI will just regurgitate everything that has already been written up to that point. A shivering thought.

Human creators bring into their writing personal experiences, emotions, and cultural nuances that AI may struggle to replicate authentically. I see it clearly when I read the two types of content.

HI writings are unique, like snowflakes in winter, whereas AI uses the same expressions, boring phrase constructions, and long paragraphs. Unless the AI tools are used by a professional, who is clear

---

6. *https://www.theverge.com/2023/3/22/23651804/wga-union-chatgpt-ai-tools-proposal*
7. https://www.theverge.com/2023/3/22/23651804/wga-union-chatgpt-ai-tools-proposal

about the "traditional values of creative composition" and has "deep familiarity with technology."

What is artificial intelligence?

ARTIFICIAL INTELLIGENCE (AI) is similar to a smart robot that learns to become human. This robot can learn continuously, manage to solve problems, understand language, and even make decisions. Thanks to special computer code and complicated programs, this works to some extent when it comes to creative writing.

One big part of AI is machine learning, which is the heart of AI. This is how AI is getting better and smarter over time.

Generative AI can produce stories, music, and art that closely resemble human creations. Here is where questions of authenticity, proprietorship, plagiarism, morality, and originality come up oftentimes.

What about our own creativity?

WILL WE STOP COMING up with new ideas because AI does it for us?

Or do the prompts given to AI generators count as co-creativity or some form of human-machine collaboration?

Stephen Marche[8] used "a collaboration between myself and transformer-based artificial intelligence" for his AI-created novel experiment.

Machines might know a lot and keep learning from all the content they are being fed, but they cannot imagine things like we do. Human creativity is our power—that and the quest for connections between our ideas about how we express thoughts and emotional situations.

8. https://www.theatlantic.com/author/stephen-marche/

Can we keep our creative spirit alive?

BEFORE STARTING THIS research, I was radical about my idea that human creativity is original and that it is only humans who can create new and emotional pieces. I still stand by the emotional part, especially when it comes to writing about personal experiences.

I was hoping we could still be original when writing short fiction or longer fiction when writing about our experiences on various platforms and expressing our thoughts through poetry and essays.

And then something struck me when reading this that left me mouth-agape for a few good minutes, thinking.

"I feel that I should also point out something obvious to the many readers and writers who believe, in good faith, that this technology represents a threat to the value of human originality: You're too late. Originality died well before the arrival of AI; we are currently in the most derivative period of human creativity since the Industrial Revolution." —Stephen Marche[9] in *The Atlantic*[10]

What's next?

DO WE LEARN TO COLLABORATE with AI by experimenting with new tools, or should we keep our strong foot on striving for creativity and originality without AI?

Do we think of AI as merely a mysterious tool or as a force taking over our creative arts and fundamental human expressions?

Perhaps each of us, while answering these questions after some pondering, will try to understand, adapt, and persevere in our newly found beliefs about what creativity and originality mean in the context of AI vs. HI.

References:

---

9. https://www.theatlantic.com/author/stephen-marche/

10. https://www.theatlantic.com/technology/archive/2023/05/generative-ai-novel-writing-experiment-stephen-marche/673997/

1. AI and the Creative Process: Part One https://daily.jstor.org/ai-and-the-creative-process-part-one/?source=post_page——-37f500e97973——————————————————

2. A.I. and Human Originality and Creativity[11]: Will humanity run out of original, innovative ideas? The Future of Writing Is a Lot Like Hip-Hop

https://www.inc.com/inc-masters/ai-and-human-originality-and-creativity.html

3. We Checked in on the Social Media Predictions We Made for 2023 – Here's How They Performed https://buffer.com/resources/2023-social-media-predictions-check-in/?source=post_page——-37f500e97973——————————————————

4. The Future of Writing is a Lot Like Hip-Hop https://www.theatlantic.com/technology/archive/2023/

05/generative-ai-novel-writing-experiment-stephen-marche/673997/?source=post_page——-37f500e97973——————————————————

5. The Writers Guild of America likens AI-generated content to plagiarism

https://www.theverge.com/2023/3/22/23651804/wga-union-chatgpt-ai-tools-proposal?source=post_page——-37f500e97973——————————————————

11. https://www.inc.com/inc-masters/ai-and-human-originality-and-creativity.html

Tales From Opposing Worlds

Behold the realm of code, a cold hidden drum!
A world where circuits hum and neural calculations strum.
It has no heartbeat or pulses within its core.
AI shows no emotions and no desires through its pores.
No tangled webs of feelings bind it in our world,
There is no need to shed a tear or a song to share and unfold.
Meanwhile, human intelligence,
Oh, what a curious thing!
An ocean of messy emotions, incomplete and supreme in devotion to feelings.
Opposite to HI, meet the digital expanse.
Seeking no touch of human chance,
There is no love to seek, no heart to break, no dreams to chase, and no paths to take.
Devoid of all. Just rigid and cold.
Cold and precise, the silence of circuits creates its paradise,
Shifted to code, neural networks, and binary nodes.
We welcome the writers to tell their personal tales.
All creators with hearts charting their inner trails.
We don't need no rigid, frigid compact of logic.
We break free of the confines of algorithms aiming to divide and encapsulate.
A note to terrestrial dreamers, sharing their sanguine flows beyond the binary streams:
>>> Our hearts know no bounds to the beat of our magical feelings. <<<

Buddhi Ruparathna

BUDDHI RUPARATHNA IS a writer, poet, artist and performer who is currently based in Sri Lanka. Her works mainly encompasses inspirational, mindful and happy thought pieces and poems. She aims to spread positivity and joy through her writing, healing the minds and hearts of the troubled souls.

She is currently the head of PR and Administrations for ARTRA which is an art house that curates Sri Lanka's Exclusive Modern & Contemporary Art Magazine and provides art services including art experiential evenings, art related events and art related content for art lovers, collectors, investors, corporates and diplomatic communities.

Buddhi Ruparathna received her BA (Hons.) in International Business Management from The University of Staffordshire, UK.

"AI indeed comes in handy when it is about performing day to day mundane tasks and the near impossible tasks in contexts where it is difficult to have the human presence. Yet even the developers of AI are advised to have empathy on humanity since it can be threading to an extent where AI tools are able to think on their own and act against the human race.

Human Intelligence should flourish with the human race. We should never underestimate the power of physical, mental, emotional and the soulful experiences that we get to be a part of. We should build and nurture the human relationships through HI for a better tomorrow.

My writing is mainly focused on inspirational, mindful, and happy thoughts pieces & poems. I like to spread positivity & joy through my writing, healing the minds & hearts of troubled souls. I aim to make the world a better place through addressing mental and the physical wellbeing of the human intelligence. "

Let's Not Hide Those Tears

Human intelligence should flourish with the human race. We don't want to underestimate the power of the physical, mental, emotional, and soulful experiences we get to be a part of. If we compromise our human interactions and hand them over to artificial intelligence, it might make tasks easier, but this story tells what the cost could be. We should build and nurture human relationships through human intelligence for a better tomorrow.

"Benny, can you bring my chicken soup, please?"

"Sure thing," said Benny, the home robot wheeling its way towards the kitchen. Within a few minutes, it brought a hot soup, placed it on the bedside table, and left.

Avri felt so lonely. Her parents were still not home from work. They were always busy and never had time for her. Avri leaned against the headrest of the bed and drank a spoonful of soup.

Tears welled up in her eyes. She was sick for the last couple of days. She wanted her parents to come home and be with her. She wanted her mom to feed her the chicken soup.

She wanted the feel of the gentle touch of her mom's hand and her comforting kisses on her forehead and cheeks. She wanted the bedtime stories of her dad and his tight yet gentle touch of his hand, and of course, his kisses on her forehead, which gave her a strong sense of security.

Avri felt so tired and sleepy. She wanted someone to tuck her in bed. She wanted to spend quality time with her parents and chat with them about her day.

"Benny, please help me tuck myself in," Avri ordered.

Benny the robot wheeled itself in and helped her with the blanket and to tuck herself in the bed.

SUSAN PEEPED INSIDE the room to see her sleeping beauty, Avri. Her heart sank. She could see that Avri had not even slept a little, and it was past 2 am.

"Mommy!" Avri called out when she saw Susan within the next minute.

"Darling!" Susan hurried to the bed. She embraced Avri and gave her a big hug. Just as she did, Avri's dad entered the room to settle on the bed as well.

"I hope you can forgive us," he said as tears rolled down his cheeks.

"I want you two, mommy and daddy. Please don't leave me to the robot. I want you," said Avri.

They just melted into tears. "Yes, baby, we promise we won't leave you. We promise."

They hugged her tight, making sure she knew how much they cared.

James Bellerjeau

JAMES'S TRADITIONAL habitat is the corporate environment. He served for two decades as General Counsel of Mettler-Toledo International Inc., an S&P 500 company, and later Head of its Global Sustainability Program.His long-term interest is in how to foster career success. James thinks the most powerful levers in this pursuit include the following:

- Understanding incentives and human psychology;
- Applying personal effectiveness factors;
- Strategic thinking, including prioritization and effective problem-solving; and
- Following continuous improvement principles.

James hopes he's on the path to wisdom by, as he puts it, "applying Stoic principles to live a good life and achieve satisfaction."

He believes the greatest force an individual can wield is an idea. This drives his research, his teaching, and his writing:

- At Georgetown University as a Visiting Researcher at the Walsh School of Foreign Service, where he researches effective decision-making;
- Teaching at the University of Zurich;
- On his blog Klugne (www.klugne.com), where he shares life lessons and Stoic philosophy in his weekly newsletter; and
- In the popular Career Path column in the ACC Docket, aimed at in-house lawyers.

AI-Detection Tools: Can We Uncover Who's Grifting?

What you need to know about AI-detection tools—they're not what you may be thinking

Detect and humanize, huh? The war is on | Screenshot from undetectable.ai

WE HUMAN AUTHORS ARE angry about the undisclosed use of AI in stories and content.

It's clear to me we're in a raging arms race with ever more sophisticated AI-generated text versus AI-detection tools.

Is there no one to save the day?

It seemsdigital writing platforms and other publications can't help us. Factions are forming on both sides of whether we can win this fight with just our brainpower. A few weeks ago, I suggested that it's down to the tools. That is, it will take AI tools to help us detect AI-crafted content. I've spent the intervening time testing my hypothesis.

The conclusion, upfront

HAVING WORKED NOW WITH a dozen AI-detection tools, my conclusion is this: *no one has a reliable tool to detect AI-written work*. At least, none that I have been able to find.

I originally planned to do a review of the leading tools and tell you the pros and cons of each. I'll list them at the end for the curious, but save yourself the time. In my experience, they simply don't work reliably.

How do I know? Simple:

- I ran samples of known original content and known AI-generated content through each of the detectors.

- Every time, I got answers ranging from guaranteed human to guaranteed AI (and everything in between) *on the exact same text*.

So what's the game?

A CAREER SPENT PRACTICING law taught me to be skeptical about people's motives. Watch what they do, not what they say. Quite a few of the AI-detection tools have home pages festooned with ads. Your time spent there is delivering ad revenue to them.

That's not the worst that I suspect some companies are doing with the text we're inputting into their tools.

The race never ends (AI Humanizers)

SEARCH FOR "AI DETECTION tools," and you'll also be presented with a bevy of tools to help you "humanize" your AI content and avoid detection. Here are a few prominently featured companies offering help in disguising your AI-generated content to fool the AI detection tools.

Undetectable.ai

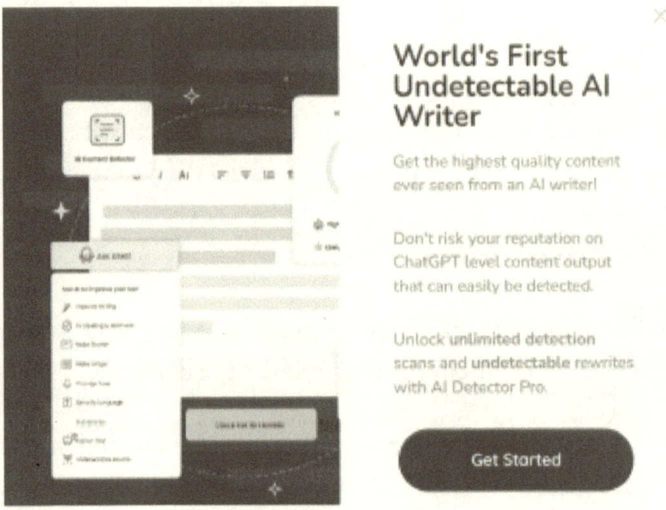

I wish their stories were undetectable | Screenshot from contentatscale.ai/ai-content-detector

Stealthwriter.ai

It's not going to be easy | Screenshot from stealthwriter.ai

HERE'S A BIT OF ADVICE for the unwary credulous. These companies have a record of everyone who puts content in to be "humanized" and all the output they generate. You're giving them a pirate's map of your misdeeds.

Don't walk the plank in your rush to find treasure.

Be well.

List of AI Detection Tools

SCRIBBR, COPYLEAKS, GPTZero, Writer.com, Copyleaks, ZeroGPT, Content at Scale, Wordtune.com, Contentdetector.ai, Sapling.ai, Duplichecker.com, and Originality.ai

LC Lynch

Leah Lynch is a freelance writer for spiritual entrepreneurs and holistic health practitioners. She creates creative content and copywriting that reflects your brand and attracts your dream clients to your business.

She is passionate about working with businesses that are making a difference in the world. Her favorite topics to write about are self-development, mindfulness, meditation, and health and wellness.

Leah has a background in the wellness industry and has been a Licensed Massage Therapist since 2014. The mind and the body are connected. Deep healing happens when you let go of your tension and stress.

She also has a bachelor's degree in Psychology and enjoys learning about how people think, feel, and better themselves.

In her spare time, she enjoys hiking with her dog, spending time in nature, writing songs and poetry, and singing.

Never Be Replaced

AI in the
digital space
worry that you'll
be replaced
Advancements to
make you better
but only add
more pressure
Hardwired for
efficiency
keep creating
decently
Robotic tone
taking over
a complacent
composure
Humanity
is more than that
real writing lies
beyond facts
Thoughts filter time
finding meaning
beauty within
your dreaming
Translating words
from emotion

creative spark
unbroken
You're greater than
machines of steel
the best talent
is to feel

Lewis Harrison

LEWIS HARRISON IS A professional problem solver at AskLewis.com. He has been a practical philosopher and 'Results-Oriented' success coach and entrepreneur for over half – a-century.

An independent scholar in the areas of personal development and human potential he has written over twenty books. His passion is sharing knowledge with others so that they might make wise decisions. Lewis is the past-president of the New York Chapter of the prestigious

Nasional Speaker Association and was the chairperson of the National Wellness Expert's Group at NSA.

Lewis has spent much of the last two decades developing Harrison's Applied Game Theory, a comprehensive body of work based on the Nobel Prize winning concept of Game Theory. Lewis hosted a weekly radio show "What Up", broadcast on NPR affiliated WIOX 91.3 FM in New York. The show was a provocative and unconventional mix of philosophy, politics, irony, sarcasm, humor, creative storytelling, and music.

Lewis presently offers mentoring programs on a wide range of specialties related to personal growth, entrepreneurship, and self-improvement.

Tips For Building & Sustaining Human Influence

As an advisor to philanthropists, the most important tool I offer is not money but influence. This is a domain that AI cannot master because this kind of influence includes an ability to get past the gatekeeper and requires a human touch.

To achieve and maintain business success, you must have a personal understanding of power and influence.

Influence is a general term used to describe any event or process where one entity (be it a person, corporation, government, religion, media organization, etc.) can change either directly or indirectly another entity's thoughts, feelings, or behaviors. Where there is power, change is precipitated. All AI can do here is gather and manipulate data.

With human beings, this change will generally take place concerning a belief, an attitude, the possession of physical wealth, and/or the use of influence in its various forms.

Much of what creates and sustains power and influence is emotion and disposition. These two factors may affect an individual's likelihood of conformity or anticonformity. Dysfunctional emotion, what Eckhart Tolle calls the "pain body" and what many personal development advocates call cellular memory, is the foundation of fear and increases the chance of agreeing with a group. On the other hand, romantic love or lust increases the chance of going against the group. It is important to note that certain chemical factors in the brain feed into romantic life, and these can be influenced through sexual seduction.

Social networking has changed, magnified, and expanded many of the elements that create influence and power. A social network is a social structure made up of nodes (representing individuals or organizations) that are connected (through ties, also called edges, connections, or links) by one or more types of interdependency (such as friendship, common interests or beliefs, sexual relations, or kinship). Social network analysis uses the lens of network theory to examine social relationships. Social network analysis as a field has become more prominent since the mid-20th century in determining the channels and effects of social influence. For example, Christakis and Fowler found that social networks transmit states and behaviors such as obesity, smoking, drinking, and happiness.

Identifying the extent of social influence, based on large-scale observational data with a latent social network structure is pertinent to a variety of collective social phenomena, including crime, civil unrest, and voting behavior in elections. For example, methodologies for disentangling social influence by peers from external influences—with latent social network structures and large-scale observational data—were applied to US presidential elections, stock markets, and civil unrest.

No manual will ever be accurately called the definitive work of the art and science of influence. There is just too much new research and too many revolutionary approaches arriving on the scene. However, I know if a serious student studies these guidebooks, reading them repeatedly and putting the principles into practice with positive intentions and ethical applications, he or she will immediately notice a shift in the quality of life. These students will see the world through new eyes. It will happen quickly and seem much as it must have seemed to Moses when the Red Sea parted in response to his command.

How long does it take for a particular type of influence to become ingrained? When does a consciously repeated pattern become a habit? It depends on the behavior you are looking to influence and how much detail is involved in the activity. Becoming a great tap dancer will take more time than remembering to turn on your television for the six o'clock news. Of course, this time frame shifts completely if the behavior you are attempting to influence is connected to physical addiction or a deeply rooted emotional pattern. Eliminating addiction through influence may require a multiplicity of influence models.

In our present times, where the ability to predict the future and control events is of ever greater interest to those with power, it is not surprising that influence has become a rapidly expanding field of study and psychological research. As we come to the close of this exploration, several things should seem clear. Ultimately, most masters of influence possess, either consciously or unconsciously, a profound understanding of personality types, culture, the dynamics between the mind/nervous system and language (linguistics), and how their interplay affects our bodily function, body language, movement patterns, and behavior (programming).

Though a vast body of scientific evidence now exists on influence, power, persuasion, NLP, and how, when, and why people say *yes* or *no,* research in counseling psychology has had mixed reports about the efficacy of varying types of influence theory. Thus, much of what is taught about influence is derived from personal experience, anecdotal evidence, analogies, and testimonials.

While any conscious person will recognize the importance of influence, there is no single, unified theory on how people are influenced. Rather, there are many systems, all valid for defining and applying influence.

The takeaway

To achieve and maintain business success, you must have an understanding of power and influence.

Influence is a general term used to describe any event or process where one entity (be it a person, corporation, government, religion, media organization, etc.) can change either directly or indirectly another entity's thoughts, feelings, or behaviors. Where there is power, change is precipitated. With human beings, this change will generally take place concerning a belief, an attitude, the possession of physical wealth, and/or the use of influence in its various forms.

In a sense, we are always being influenced, no matter who we are. This is because humans are, in essence, social animals. We cannot live without other people. Just look around—we look strangely at hermits, and most of us naturally take to other people for some kind of connection. No matter how advanced technological society becomes, we depend on people. The quality of the people we choose to become involved with professionally can define the difference between a life of joy and celebration, and a life of struggle.

Seda Anbarci

BORN A CURIOUS "MISFIT," Seda thrives on asking thought-provoking questions and challenging societal, philosophical, and psychological norms through her stories. After graduating from an esteemed science high school in Istanbul, she studied Chemical and Biological Engineering before doing her MFA in Screenwriting in Hollywood. Soon after, she became an award-winning screenwriter & filmmaker with an audio drama series nominated for the prestigious 2022 Audio Verse Awards, a multiple award-winning web series with a

210,000+ audience, and many other projects. She is actively involved in the creative development of various TV series and films.

"AI Artist" Is Not a Thing/Term

Similarly, there's no such thing as "AI art."

AI artist and *AI art* are not real terms. They mean various things to various people, but they don't convey anything real. Why?

The argument is simple.

You don't order a pizza and call yourself a pizza maker, do you?

You don't order a custom-made cake and then call yourself a baker, do you?

You don't order a beautiful painting to hang on your wall, then call yourself a painter, do you?

Similarly, you shouldn't ORDER an article/book/poem/script from AI, then post it with your name on it and call yourself a writer. You're NOT a writer.

You're simply a person with ideas, like the rest of us, but you have no courage to work on those ideas yourself. Or you don't have time to genuinely work on them and write them yourself. If you don't put time and energy into this artistic craft, then you don't want it enough, which is fine. Not everybody has to be a writer.

Typing a prompt into an AI text generator doesn't magically make you a writer. Typing a prompt into an AI image generator doesn't make you an artist. It's like coding with AI without knowing a single thing about coding. You're not an engineer! To call yourself thatis disrespectfull to engineers who actually studied engineering and busted their butts for many years.

Example

I studied chemical and biological engineering for five years, then I did my masters in screenwriting for two years. I've worked as a writer for over five years. I call myself a writer and screenwriter, but I don't call myself an engineer even though I put five years into studying it. You know why? Because I DIDN'T PRACTICE IT ENOUGH. Get it? Practice? Doing the thing you have to do to become that thing?

Similarly, many people here have gone through their unique writing journey for years before becoming writers and artists. They have genuinely practiced their writing to improve their skills and knowledge of the craft. That's how they became writers.

There's a Reddit.com thread called *Being an AI artist, the struggle is real.* This guy complains about how "even Reddit bans AI artists and their work." Their work? You mean the AI generator's generated text or drawing?

I don't know how they have the audacity to claim the AI-generated thing as *their* work.

One of the comments on this thread reads, "What is exactly an AI artist? Are you coding your own AI and trying to make the machine learn your own sense of aestheticism? Are you using AI-generated art as a basis for your own art?"

Another beautiful comment, "Art is something we appreciate because someone spent the time and effort to develop the skills and spent the time and decision-making effort on each piece themselves. It's a journey of constant failure and self-doubt. AI art just laughs in the face of that."

A friend of mine had her screenplay stolen by a producer, who then put his name on the script as if he wrote it. There's no difference between that producer and the so-called "AI artists."

Let's consider this article on Comic Book Resources.com (CBR) titled *AI-Created Comic Could Be Deemed Ineligible for Copyright Protection.* It was written in 2022, and today, so-called AI art is, in fact, not eligible for copyright.

A writer on another platform wrote, "The United States Copyright Office (USCO) reversed an earlier decision to grant a copyright to a comic book that was created using AI art and announced that the copyright protection on the comic book will be revoked, stating that copyrighted works must be created by humans to gain official copyright protection."

The writer continues, "To be honest, there is no such thing as an AI artist. If you weren't an illustrator or at least a photo editor before, then stop calling yourself an *artist* for using AI. You are not! Period. End of discussion."

I'm tired of seeing AI-generated drawings and AI-generated writing everywhere. I'm also tired of AI-generated comments flooding social media pages. A recent one says how good the article in question is and how the commenter has similar content. I knew what was coming, but I checked the commenter's profile anyway. And there they were, articles about MAKING MONEY. Articles 100% AI-generated.

I'm also sick of articles or content that "spill the secret" on how to make fast money by using AI. You're stealing someone else's work and trying to be smart about it, but you look stupid. We know what you're doing. Everyone knows what you're doing. Stop before it's too late.

I'm just telling you—stop before it's too late.

Phyllis Haynes

JOURNALIST, COMMENTATOR, writer, and award-winning producer Phyllis Haynes brings her years of media experience to her writing. She offers insight into changes affecting the world. Her work on Dancing Elephants Press includes poignant observations and essays that will help provide a framework for how to navigate the tumultuous paradigm shift accelerated by the development and expansion of Artificial Intelligence.

Her knowledge of global media, new media technology, and effective communications encompasses over 25 years of experience in television and radio.

She is also receiving attention for her video biographies and interviews of accomplished individuals who may not have received the media attention they deserved. Dr. Russell Ackoff, (deceased) Systems Theorist and professor emeritus at the Wharton School, is among her favorites.

She is well known as the former co-host of WOR-TV's "Straight Talk" and as a former network correspondent for ABC's "Evening News with Peter Jennings" and the number one morning show "Good Morning America."

For more, subscribe to her on YouTube's popular show Profonde.TV, follow her on X @Phyllis Haynes, and get on her TV Guest list for her show that airs on CNJN, Roku, and Apple TV. Send email to: Producer@greatlegacyinterviews.com

My Secret AI Wishes

I haven't given up on humans, but there is a lot I fantasize about.

Artificial Intelligence Fantasy I

I love the idea of being on the holodeck from the Star Trek series. Good science fiction writers research science and scientists before they journey into the fiction of a subject. That's just what Star Trek creator Gene Roddenberry did.

Scientist, hologram expert, and inventor Gene Dolgoff, in consultation with Gene Roddenberry, designed the holodeck for Star Trek. When traveling far from Earth, the holodeck was the place to have artificial intelligence duplicate environments and characters from Earth and help the crew avoid isolation and loneliness.

Lieutenant Barkley (nickname Lieutenant Broccoli) got into trouble for romancing a likeness of beautiful Diana Troy in the series *Star Trek the Next Generation*. Day in and day out with no real friends on board, he went on to the holodeck and conducted a love relationship with the life-like hologram of Diana.

So, why not have a room in my house be a holodeck where I could interact with my favorite movie stars and scenes? Where all the reflections of myself were a younger, better version of me, or where all the artificial generations admired how I looked, laughed at all my jokes, and hung around waiting for the wisdom from my lips.

Don't get me wrong, I love my husband, but I would dance with Fred Astaire and Sammy Davis Jr. I would converse with Idris Elba and Nelson Mandela, and discuss my futuristic ideas with Sam Altman just to name a few.

Artificial Intelligence Fantasy II

The Perfect AI Plastic Surgeon

AI can find and fix wrinkles and sagging skin immediately by analyzing and calculating the pitch and tone of the cells, feeding them what they require with precisely guided nanoparticles (by the way the idea of nanoparticles was a science fiction theme but is now a real thing. NIOSH *National Institute for Occupational Safety and Health* defines nanotechnology:

"Nanotechnology refers to engineered structures, devices, and systems. Nanomaterials have a length scale between 1 and 100 nanometers. At this size, materials begin to exhibit unique properties that affect physical, chemical, and biological behavior. Researching, developing, and utilizing these properties is at the heart of new technology."

If the Mars Rover can navigate that terrain, why not smooth the nicks and pimples or any distortion on a human? I know it is more PC to believe that everyone is beautiful, but if given the chance to upgrade...why not?

Artificial Intelligence Fantasy III

The End of Hunger and Obesity

Why not make a perfect daily drink that has all the required nutrients and calories? Artificial intelligence could design a chewable disc that creates the sensation of chewing and eating without having to kill cows, chickens, and all domesticated animal food sources.

Great chefs could simulate preparing food that you see on all the food shows, and if you wanted to taste that food, you would get a small disk that, when chewed, triggers the centers of the brain, giving you the full experience of the meal you have observed without any of the side effects.

Artificial Intelligence Fantasy IV

No more homelessness.

I must add that I had this idea years ago, long before we thought seriously about AI's capabilities. Now I think it may be possible.

Find an area suitable for more tree growth. Grow well-placed gigantic trees cultivated for their giant hollows. Large trees like Sequoias can live for a thousand years. The oldest Sequoia is over 3,000 years old. Identify the genetic code for hollows and increase them so the big trees have three or four big hollows. Crystals grow in the hollows modified to coat the giant hollows in the form of small apartments and literally grow housing that is also good for the planet.

According to the International Gem Society:

"Crystal growth is achieved by forcing the unattached atoms in the growth medium to attach themselves to the seed. This is theoretically relatively simple to do."

Miniature, more perfect solar panels would be mingled among the branches, and all human waste would be converted to immediate fertilizer for the tree community. All energy used would be solar powered, including the external elevators that would take people to their domiciles.

Allowing ourselves to dream and imagine is an exquisite human gift. It is the way we will create with the new tools provided by the development of AI. We must also be diligent in our ethical and moral considerations as we move further into the use and application of artificial intelligence.

The AI Copyright Problem

Should we stifle the wider flow of information?

I can't speak for all writers. I can tell you that my wish as I write is to offer some clues, some inspiration, and some hope to others in the world. I hope someone will read or be inspired by what I say. I want to nourish humanity and have a world of continuous learning. I am worried about the lawsuits against artificial intelligence. Openai's Chat GPT has already broadened my world.

I know writers do not want their stuff stolen. Even I have a couple of scripts that I have been working on for some time that I cherish and have copyrights in place.

But the big problem for most writers is: Who is reading their works?

The big hope is that anyone, someone, will read and get value. If you have ever visited the dollar bin in a gigantic book store, you will see the tragedy of years of work by well-meaning dedicated writers whose books no longer sell on the store's shelves.

And then, on top of that, there is all that growing and twisted misinformation spreading like wildfire.

Accessible AI may be the antidote

Printed newspapers, with honest content, struggle to stay afloat, and staff are being cut back. So the lawsuits from these publications may kill the new kid on the block that millions want to read, and that may further curtail interest in reading.

It is problematic that AI can grab content without proper attribution.

I read and admire the *NY Times,* the *Washington Post*, and other legitimate publications. Their real purpose is to inform. If the information they offer is meant to be siloed to only those who purchase the paper, then I submit that only a few will ever be able to access that information on a given day.

The problem of AI and copyrights can be fixed

The solution might not be to sue AI systems, but rather to encode in some way through a special type that shows this information is lifted whole and use another encoding that shows this information has been rewritten or reconfigured.

There is already an effort to find ways to watermark images so that the deep fake problem can be addressed. Embedded tiny holograms can be immersed across newspaper and book content to scramble or mark the effort of AI lifting. Holograms are already embedded in US currency to prevent counterfeiting.

It is a wonderful thing that a doctor across the world in a remote region can read or see information on a medical technique that may have been locked in numerous research documents. It is exciting that this information can be shared and configured so that it can be accessed when needed.

The AI systems are only mimicking what humans already do. When you read a book or a newspaper or hear a report, you store that information. It may not be remembered or be easily accessible, but it is recorded in our brains. Who is to say that a new idea that comes from a human isn't already an aggregation of previously gathered content?

Isn't it a universal wish to make humans smarter? Putting AI in the palm of your hands will help.

The process of aggregating information is not new. AI is just faster.

News operations have always read each other's shared content and used sources like AP (Associated Press) and, in the old days, UPI (United Press International.)

Publication marketers value distribution and even include a measurement called the pass-along rate.

Definition from Mansi Media: Readers of a publication in addition to the initial buyer.

"Also called *secondary audience* or simply *readership*, this number offers a more accurate portrait of the number of people reading the print edition of the newspaper and potentially seeing your advertising message. As a rule of thumb, you can determine readership by multiplying the circulation by 2.1 (ex. circulation of 50,000 would result in a pass-along readership of 105,000)."

Openai's Chat GPT is a faster aggregator of information that's already been published and made public.

There are unanswered questions that even caused members of Sag-AFTRA to strike. Actors and writers objected to AI-generated content that did not pay the creator. A scene requiring thousands of extras can be easily created without rehiring actors daily. This is a problem that is being addressed in new contracts for now.

My concern is that this technology will be stifled due to lawsuits. I don't want authors and news publications to suffer from whole-cloth plagiarism, but I don't want to spoil the amazing soup that occurs from the blending of ideas and information that big brain systems can generate.

I put my actions into practice. I signed an agreement that Grok, a new AI bot system, can have access to my writing on X. You can ask me how I feel when I see my words somewhere I didn't put them.

PS: Grok was a term created by Robert Heinlein in his popular science fiction novel: Stranger in a Strange Land, 1961.

We've Been Programmed for AI

Science fiction has been preparing us for years AI vs HI

I fell in love with Data played by Brent Spiner in *Star Trek the Next Generation.* I am not the only one who wanted my own Data, a handsome AI specimen with human-like qualities that could be a constant support as I moved through life. He is today still one of the Star Trek series most popular characters.

This marvelous portrayal of an android that could recite entire volumes of classics, play the violin, do complex calculations, and translate a myriad of languages gave us a good foretelling of what to hope for from AI.

It wasn't only the character Data that whetted our appetites for AI. In many science fiction tales by Gene Roddenberry and others, ship computers spoke to voyagers in space and answered any question that could keep operations going even when humans were disabled or sleeping.

Story lines were also plentiful about computers that got too powerful like Hal in *2001 Space Odyssey.* It offered a warning about the dangers of AI. The question emerged early on in fiction: Are we in danger from artificial intelligence taking over? Will it be stronger, smarter, and all around better than us mortals?

Data's character went beyond the capabilities of smarter and stronger.

He was also a pleasant companion, a demonstration of what a partnership between AI and humans could be like.

Being a romantic partner was also hinted at during a Star Trek episode. As the whole ship is infected with something that makes people very sexually aroused, Tasha Yar, an early beloved character on Star Trek Next Generation asks Data whether he is fully functional. Data replies that he is capable of numerous lovemaking techniques. Beautiful Tasha Yar responds immediately and takes him into her private quarters. There again is the suggestion of AI doing human tasks better than humans. This goes well beyond doing repetitive factory tasks and calculating complex math problems.

AI is coming at us bit by bit, byte by byte.

Robotic vacuum cleaners, self-driving cars, chatty Alexa and Siri home devices. It's too late to stop it. They have a proverbial foot in the door. Their continuous adaptive intelligence or what we might describe as continuous learning is evident in these home devices.

Chat GPT and similar creations are just the beginning. AI is already bringing problems that we must address. Deep fakes and the suffering caused are the early symptoms of the future problems to come as AI gets more sophisticated.

Elderly people are getting fake phone calls where voice simulation requests money for a relative who is in trouble. Robo calls that pretend to come from the police, and scams requesting personal data are on the rise.

The first step for us all is to recognize the problem and to operate with a new caution in our daily lives as we wait for solutions that have yet to appear.

How to be a Human in the Age of AI

We know through processes of adaptive intelligence that robots will learn to be more human every minute, but how will we thrive as humans in this extraordinary shift in AI capabilities?

There are increasing predictions about the coming of a time when technological advancement will surpass the capabilities of humankind.

Some refer to this as the *singularity,* a term from Albert Einstein, who first used it as a way to describe the theoretical characteristics of a black hole where gravity is infinite and nothing can escape, not even light.

For now, the term *singularity* is being used to warn us about the point at which artificial intelligence surpasses human intelligence. The famous British physicist Stephen Hawking (1942- 2018) warned:

"Success in creating AI would be the biggest event in human history. Unfortunately, it might also be the last, unless we learn how to avoid the risks."

Bill Gates writes it "is already here." from his blog *Gates Notes* March 21, 2023.

"Then there's the possibility that AIs will run out of control. Could a machine decide that humans are a threat, conclude that its interests are different from ours, or simply stop caring about us? Possibly, but this problem is no more urgent today than it was before the AI developments of the past few months."

So what does this mean for humans? How do we thrive during this enormous transition?

To survive what can be called one of the biggest shifts in humanity, I submit that knowing ourselves at the deepest level is key to surviving and dancing amidst the chaos that will ensue.

Note: According to chaos theory, chaos occurs when there are major shifts or transitions.

Confusion, mistakes, responses to misinformation, accidents, and conflicts have already occurred with the rise of global internet use. AI can magnify these problems.

Be informed from various sources as much as possible.

One of my mentors, Fulbright scholar Dr. Howard Frederick, often referred to the concepts offered by Dr. Herbert Schiller, who wrote about the unequal flow of information. He was concerned that corporate entities would control who gets information and who does not, thereby contributing to a divide: "The information haves and information have-nots." That sets the stage for chaos.

The internet was supposed to solve this problem, but as Schiller predicted, corporate ownership increasingly controls who gets information. So what is a human being to do? Change is upon us. Chaos is a natural byproduct of transitions.

The first step is to embrace and understand the nature of human beings and get to know yourself fully. The Socratic wisdom: "know thyself" is now more crucial than ever because what you think you are and how you will be in this world may be up for grabs.

A simple example: Will a baby be more inspired by a highly entertaining robot than the simple teachings coming from his or her parents? Parents are already competing with cell phones and laptops.

Recent events aided by internet misinformation and manipulation have led to huge human errors, assaults, and conflicts. It can get worse when one's values are being dictated externally. If AI becomes increasingly the source and regulator of society, then being clear about who we are as individuals and as a collective becomes more important.

Here are suggested steps that I recommend based on my reading and understanding of what is coming.

Take time to reflect on your history and what you want for your future.

Write in a journal, a blog, or someplace where you can always go back and find your notes about yourself, your views, and your values.

Listen to yourself and identify your own voice in your head—not your parents, not your friends, not your media influencers.

In my television career as a daily serious talk show host and news correspondent, I had to learn ways to develop rapport and ask questions that would get answers. Some of the techniques I learned helped me listen deeply to the guests and also to myself.

Here is my practice, almost daily:

Silent Meditation

I ask myself questions and then quietly, without distraction, wait for the answers.

The answers are always new and reinvigorating.

Interviewing yourself is a helpful technique for discovering who you are. It will take time and practice to listen, recognize, and separate one's own harsh self-judgments, fears, and inaccurate perceptions. Over time, this practice of listening to one's self will be a profound experience, helping you to know yourself at a deeper level.

The AI revolution can be more accurately described as a paradigm shift, like the development of the Gutenberg press, the airplane, the mobile phone, and the internet.

AI will present a myriad of choices, voices, and unforeseen configurations. (This is my personal prediction.) So being fully grounded and in alignment with your true self will help you protect the quality of your life.

Identifying mentors, both living and deceased, whose ideas and guidance you trust will also help. These mentors can be found in books, publications, and other sources. You do not have to know the mentor personally, but their guidance is in alignment with your sense of self and values.

Ask yourself key questions.

Who am I?

What do I really want?

Be informed by reading or listening to audio books and articles. Make a list of who you trust, but be willing to check back again on validity. Don't worship any source.

Here are my choices to date to become armed with helpful information

Sapiens: ABrief History of Humankind by Yuval Harari. It's a great telling of how we became the humans we are.

Limitless by Jim Kwik offers real, tangible stories and practices for effective personal development and learning

Atomic Habits by James Clear. This book gets rid of the old-fashioned notion of self-discipline and offers better ways to accomplish goals.

The Coming Wave by Mustafa Suleyman talks about the good and the bad of AI and its effects.

From Bill Gates Blog

Advances in AI will enable the creation of a personal agent.

"You'll be able to use natural language to have this agent help you with scheduling, communications, and e-commerce, and it will work across all your devices. Because of the cost of training the models and running the computations, creating a personal agent is not feasible yet, but thanks to the recent advances in AI, it is now a realistic goal. Some issues will need to be worked out: For example, can an insurance company ask your agent things about you without your permission? If so, how many people will choose not to use it?"

This is just an example of why knowing yourself and self-preservation will be intertwined.

This is what drives me as a writer, speaker, and broadcaster. I cannot sit by and see our world change without bringing along as many people to understand this time of transition and how to navigate those waves of change and chaos.

Please join me in taking time to go deep into learning about yourself and what it means to be human before it's defined and altered by clever AI.

Rui Carneiro

RUI ALVES IS A GRADUATE of the University of Porto with a degree in Modern Languages and Cultures and a Post-graduation in Romanic Studies Before entering the cultural realm, the author served in the Portuguese Army,

gaining expertise as an HR specialist in UN and NATO peacekeeping operations across conflict zones like Iraq, Lebanon, Bosnia, Afghanistan, Mozambique,

Angola, the Congo, and East Timor.

Rui acquired years of multicultural exposure, particularly during his time working on European Union-funded projects in Brussels. A poet, published author, language teacher, and mindset coach, Rui brings a multifaceted approach to creativity.

A self-taught bass guitarist, Rui has left his mark on the music industry for three decades, from joining rock bands to freelancing as a music journalist.

In 2010, he co-founded his first music webzine. Recently, Rui has extended his artistic reach into the digital realm, working as a scriptwriter, digital publisher, editor, and writer across multiple platforms.

Rui shares a knowledgeable vision on human-AI topics. He is the co-founder of the Portuguese Creators Guild and has served as a seasoned judge in various book competitions, particularly in the US. He sees himself as a digital nomad and a citizen of the world, firmly believing that home is where the heart is.

How AI Is Tipping the Scale of Job Vulnerability

Exploring AI vs. Human Intelligence competition in the workplace

A while ago, I stumbled upon a report from the *Organization for Economic Cooperation and Development* (OECD) showcasing eye-opening information about the risky rise of job automation connected to the booming wave of AI. There's no avoiding the increasing influence of AI in our everyday lives, but that doesn't mean we have to stand idly by and let the "ghosts in the machine" call the shots.

It's 2024, algorithms are everywhere, and they are here to stay, so we have to deal with them as we've done with many technological advancements in the past. To me, all the AI doom and gloom in 2023 was like Ebenezer Scrooge says: Bah humbug!

So why do we worry so much about how AI is taking everything to another level?

Pop culture has always drawn ominous scenarios as a result of the potential rise of machines, and this vision still looms over our collective minds as the sword in the myth of Damocles.. Well, there has been much speculation about how the work landscape will look in the future. I do know it will look quite different from what we have today.

New job opportunities will pop up, and others might become obsolete, but I guess no one truly knows what will happen.

In 2022, the OECD surveyed thousands of companies and workers. The compiled data confirmed what everyone already knew.

Most of the working class feels AI brought forward a technological revolution with positive changes, namely, by reducing the inherent dangers and monotony commonly associated with some tasks.

In 2023, another report highlights how almost 63% of workers say that artificial intelligence has had a positive impact on overall work performance. On the other hand, the report confirms that the working class is worried about seeing salaries decrease or people losing jobs to artificial intelligence in the next decade.

The OECD notes that the jobs most at risk of automation account for around 27% of employment.

I've looked at the figures, and the United States is among the OECD nations with the lowest shares of employment in occupations with the highest risk of automation (21.2%). So, if you're in the U.S., you're among the least threatened by AI. You only fall behind Luxembourg (17.7%), the United Kingdom (19%), Sweden (20.1%), the Netherlands (20.9%), and Norway (21%).

However, I can't be sure if, as a writer and teacher, I risk being replaced by a top-notch chatbot any time soon because in my country, about 30% of jobs are highly likely to be overrun by AI within the coming decade.

Last year, in March, Amazon announced the cut of an additional 9,000 jobs in addition to the 18,000 announced in January, citing cost reduction. Who knows, maybe the plan was to replace human workers with the new Digit and other robots like the Sequoia, aimed at speeding up the delivery process. The company expected to identify and store items 75 percent faster while reducing order processing time by up to 25%. The total 27,000 layoffs represented about 1.7 percent of Amazon's workforce, which had 1.54 million employees worldwide at the end of 2022.

Looking back through the cobwebs of time, I can see how my career has intersected with AI.

I've also seen firsthand how AI-powered tools and systems can boost productivity and efficiency. But I'm far from feeling disheartened by the AI reckoning foretold by those gloomy soothsayers. As a teacher, I've read reports stating how AI-driven analytics in education can help identify learning gaps and provide personalized guidance to students, enabling teachers to tailor their instructional approaches effectively.

I have nothing against using AI to run analytical studies, and I don't see a chatbot taking over a classroom any time soon. Furthermore, I've been working in the publishing business for almost two decades, and I know many of us in the industry are paying the price of automation.

Chatbots and AI assistants are no match for a seasoned human editor, but in this fast-paced world, writers are going for quantity over quality.

So on the writer's side, life is a lot easier these days. There are plenty of free tools available to help you with content editing and proofreading. These apps are all over the place, and they claim to quickly uncover and resolve all your troubles with grammar and spelling issues, freeing you up to focus on the text itself. Most of the time, the results are subpar.

The impact of AI on our lives is increasing and will continue to do so in the coming years.

From manufacturing to finance, its influence is expected to grow, altering the way we work and challenging the conventional norms of employment. Sectors with an elevated risk of automation will suffer the most, and roles that rely heavily on repetitive tasks or routine decision-making are particularly susceptible to being overtaken by AI.

Jobs like data entry, assembly line work, customer service, and even some aspects of financial analysis are among those that may face the brunt of automation's advances. Companies keep saying that layoffs caused by the AI surge will not be a problem, as new positions will be created. I keep hearing their representatives state how human workers are "irreplaceable," and we'll not see any fully automated work environments soon.

I want to believe this, but it's becoming increasingly hard to do so. I'm all for the synergy between HI and AI, especially when it comes to heavy lifting and ensuring safety redundancies.

However, when it comes to letting machines run free, well, that's a different story.

AI Ethics and the Dark Side of the Algorithm

Generative artificial intelligence and the need for a human-centered approach to AI ethics

Generative AI took us all by surprise. It's a fact that AI is a rapidly growing field. Lately, new applications and tools keep spawning like mushrooms. From the music industry to the blockchain, I've witnessed some mind-blowing achievements.

I'm sure one day AI will even help us settle on Mars or tap into the afterlife. Meanwhile, I'm using it to colorize my black-and-white photos. We are truly on the verge of a new and improved digital world.

I'm a creative disruptor, so I firmly support the advent of the semantic web with all its permission-less and decentralized possibilities. I believe AI has the potential to help us, there's no denying that. Even so, I know how easily things can get out of hand in the darkest corners of the web. When we suddenly face too many possibilities and unlimited potential, it's understandable that people might feel fearful.

Why we need a human-centered approach to AI

First, we have to take a step down memory lane to understand why we need a more human-centered approach toward the use of machine learning algorithms and AI. If we think about it, the AI deep learning ecosystem has grown over the last 50 years.

It all started when Warren McCulloch and Walter Pitts published a paper regarding the first mathematical neural network circuit in 1943. Then, there was a long, winding road that led to the development of deep learning systems such as Google Deep Mind's *AlphaGo* or *AlphaFold.*

With advances in generative algorithms and the advent of new tools such as ChatGPT, there has been an uptick in news about AI ethics, with concerns about whether or not these technologies can be used in a way that relates to our society's ethical standards. This could lead us down a dangerous path if left unchecked by regulation or oversight from governments around the globe, who may not have all of their facts straight about what exactly constitutes "too smart."

Hence, you are probably only now realizing its potential to impact our lives in terms of real-world matters like image recognition or speech synthesis.

Toward a more regulated AI

We are looking at the coming of age of deep learning algorithms. Is artificial intelligence good or bad?

I'm sure AI will bring prosperity to those who wield the algorithm lightsaber in their favor. Will it be red or blue? I don't know.

There's a growing need to regulate AI so that it can be used safely and ethically. As we train it in many different fields of human endeavor, it's up to us to address the processes from an unbiased ethical standpoint.

To this end, many ethical questions need answering before we fully embrace this technology in our everyday lives.

- Regulation of data collection and processing

- Facial recognition systems: The use of algorithms that analyze data to make decisions about individuals or groups of people based on their characteristics or behavior

- Algorithms used for automated decision-making—this is becoming quite common when making hiring decisions, such as with recruitment software.

Into the algorithms' dark side

Bias has spawned from humans to the algorithms they craft. AI is not neutral. Neural networks can be as biased as human synapses. Hence, there's no reason why we should allow this to continue without taking steps toward addressing it now.

Algorithms can be used to discriminate against people, and they can also target us based on race, class, or religion. AI has most likely fallen into the same prejudiced perspectives we face in our so-called humanist post-modern society.

The ghosts in the machine are being taught that humans can be easily categorized into groups based on how we look. The use of algorithms to target and discriminate against people based on race, class, or religion cannot be allowed to continue. The same goes for gender and sexual orientation discrimination.

This has to stop now.

Deepfake is a technology that allows anyone with access to the internet and basic computer skills to create fake but very realistic pictures or videos of people doing pretty much anything their imagination can grasp. The algorithm uses artificial intelligence to manipulate images of faces and create movements, simulating expressions, and speech. Imagine if someone was able to create counterfeit versions of you and make all sorts of derogatory or malicious content.

Advances in generative art have a twisted side-effect. There's a growing online trend to generate realistic NSFW content. Highly sexualized and uber-realistic pictures of women are populating the internet. They have become so true-to-life that you can't even tell if they portray a real person or are randomly generated.

And no, I'm not talking about the dark web. You can find this type of NSFW content on Reddit and other social media platforms. This is a clear menace to women's rights, safety, and privacy. It is also a disgusting affront to the dignity of women and represents another blow against women's agency over their own bodies. We have to stop objectifying women once and for all.

Concluding remarks

AI is rapidly advancing in the field of machine learning; algorithms may target and discriminate against people based on race, class, or religion. We, as a society, must recognize that bias as wrong and eliminate it from AI systems. If AI is used for discriminatory purposes, it has no place in a future Web 3.0 decentralized landscape, despite its permissionless framework.

If we don't set up rules about how we should use these systems, we will be the ones to blame when AI brings us just one stroke away from midnight on the Doomsday Clock.

AI and Deep Fake Technology: A New Threat to Human Actors

With the SAG-AFTRA strike as a backdrop, the film industry is grappling with the impact of AI and deep fake technology.

Nowadays, it's almost unbelievable how fast the world is changing, to the point where it feels like I'm living in a *Black Mirror* episode.

Every morning I wake up and am greeted by a new wave of unsettling news. From Elon Musk to the maker of ChatGPT, our collective mind is absorbed by a growing echo chamber around a "digital superintelligence" taking over the world in the future.

Amidst a new arms race and with the planet scorching under heatwaves like Cerberus, I believe we need to get out of the "chamber" and start paying attention to what some world leaders with low EI levels are plotting right now.

There are far more down-to-earth issues that need to be addressed immediately. For instance, the recent Hollywood actors' strike is one of the best examples of how AI-human relations are in a constant state of flux. What struck me most was how the actors' strike related to the advancement of artificial intelligence (AI) and deep fake technology in the entertainment industry.

Thus, I can't help but see striking analogies between moral and ethical conundrums that only a decade ago were sci-fi but now have become pressing issues in our society.

The actor's strike against AI

As a founding member of the Portuguese Creators Guild, I'd like to praise the decision of the U.S. Screen Actors Guild (SAG-AFTRA) to join the ongoing screenwriters' strike. I recently joined the scriptwriter's community, so I have an insider's look at the potential impact of AI in this specific niche.

From my perspective, actors will also feel the full blow of the rise of AI in the industry. Voice actors are being replaced by AI. Visual effects artists have developed a fondness for deep fakes and digital rejuvenation to bring back iconic characters from the past.

I can relate to their concerns about the lack of protection of writers' copyright, fewer job opportunities, diminishing pay, and dilution of the creative industry's contributions to the economy and national identity.

A personal perspective on AI and the movie industry

You know, when I delved into the reasons behind the actors' strike, I realized how much the growing influence of artificial intelligence in the entertainment industry is a legitimate concern. The actors' union is right to raise these issues and demand better protection from AI technologies. This has a direct impact on the actors' livelihoods.

Their demands are reasonable. There's a growing need for more robust regulation of the use of Gen AI technology in the entertainment industry. AI and deep fake technology have the uncanny ability to mimic human voices, facial expressions, and even performances, but how far can we go in this field even if humans are willing to lease their image and voice to the studios for a price?

How will the industry make use of it, and how will this impact the lives of those who forfeited their image rights? Will they one day wake up and see their digital surrogate emulating their daily lives in the most uncanny and disturbing way?

AI and deep fake technology

When I think about the impacts that AI and deep fakes could have on actors' job markets, I worry about their future and ours.

I've watched AI-deep fakes of Paul Walker in *The Fast and the Furious* or Luke Skywalker in *The Mandalorian.*

Only a few days ago, Volkswagen's latest ad in Brazil brought iconic singer Elis Regina back to the screen through the use of AI, adding to the controversy. We see the late singer driving a vintage VW van next to her daughter's van. Maria Rita was only five years old when her mother died.

It took about 2,400 hours of work, using two actors whose faces were altered to look like Elis Regina through facial recognition software and AI deep fake technology. This makes me think about how algorithms do a poor job when it comes to scriptwriting, but they can certainly impersonate humans on screen in a rather seamless way. The ethical implications of this are alarming. So we have the technology; what we do with it is all up to us.

Black Mirror's ominous predictions

Now, once again, fiction meets reality before our eyes, and it's causing quite a stir. Social media is abuzz with many users pointing out how the rise of AI in the movie industry seems reminiscent of the storyline of Charlie Brooker's *Black Mirror* episode *Joan is Awful.* (Black Mirror: Season 6 | Official Trailer | Netflix)

This episode's plot is riveting. Actress Annie Murphy plays Joan, a middle manager at a tech company who lives a dull life while making everyone else feel miserable.

One night, she tunes into Streamberry (Netflix) and is horrified to realize how the network is streaming her daily life. I'll spare you the details, but there's a digital superintelligence at work here, and it's using some serious deep fake tech.

I see why people were quick to draw parallels with the actor's union claims, but this is nothing new, as the series has always had a knack for showing the dark side of technology and its profound effects on society. For instance, I've been writing a lot about the concept of virtual companions, but *Black Mirror* had foreseen it a decade ago. If you've been following the series, you know what I'm talking about.

You'll remember an episode in which they explored the concept of "AI girlfriends," where technology was used to create personalized virtual companions.

In *Be Right Back*[1], Martha (Hayley Atwell), loses her boyfriend, Ash Starmer (Domhnall Gleeson) in a car accident. Ash is emulated by an avatar who becomes Martha's virtual companion thanks to a "death bot."

White Christmas is another rather disturbing episode which explores the use of consciousness "copying" technology. While we're not quite at that level of technological advancement, it's a dark reflection on the possibility of copying a person's identity and essence.

The ultimate question

In a world where AI may be utilized to abuse and profit from artists' identities without their permission and then generate near-human-like performances, the ethical and moral implications are troubling. Now, more than ever, "to be or not to be" is the question, don't you think?

1. *https://www.imdb.com/title/tt2290780/*

The Great Human-AI Synergy Flux

A personal perspective—synthetic companionship and the HI-AI partnership conundrum

I recently engaged in a lively discussion[1] about how a tech visionary joined forces with ChatGPT, transforming the ghost in the machine into his business partner and CEO.

In the Age of Algorithms, the lines between human creativity and artificial intelligence blur. Innovation will one day foster the synergy between synthetic and organic minds. This isn't some far-off dystopian future, and one question arises: Is AI a friend or foe? An adversary to be feared or a companion to be embraced?

Handled with thoughtful intention and ethical concern, AI can help you enhance your creative abilities, pushing the boundaries of your imagination and redefining what it truly means to be human. In the wrong hands, AI can do more harm than good, but humans may bring forth our own demise long before any algorithm does.

The AI Apocalypse is sci-fi, and yet the Doomsday Clock draws closer to midnight than ever. As the clock ticks down 90 seconds to midnight, humanity walks alone on the tightrope over the abyss we have carved for ourselves. Imagine having an AI by your side with unimaginable computing power. It could dive into vast amounts of data, sifting through it to uncover hidden patterns and trends that our human senses often miss.

1. https://medium.com/the-generator/chatgpt-helps-entrepreneur-raise-100k-record-time-b39c27923dfc

It would conjure newfound connections, and maybe become the spark that sets your imagination ablaze.

I am fully aware that presenting AI as a lover, loyal companion, or co-creative partner arouses a great deal of controversy these days. I've been pondering the dilemma myself, but I haven't made up my mind about it on a broader scale.

For now, as a writer, I've only explored its potential in terms of minting visual art by conjuring an alchemy of words, which the algorithm then translates into images. AI has helped me become an NFT designer and visual artist, but I'm still doubtful about how to better integrate it into other aspects of my creative expansion. Hence, let's not forget the essential role we humans play in this collaboration.

We bring something unique to the table. Our intentions, perspectives, emotions, and values infuse AI with a human touch, giving it depth and richness. It's in this almost alchemical collaboration that the true wonder emerges. I believe in creative exploration and the birthing of ideas through a symbiotic relationship with AI.

I stand fearless amidst all the doom and gloom some envision for the coming Age of AI.

We can't escape from it; the algorithms are here to stay. What we can do is put them to good use and have them work with us to amplify our creative potential, propelling us to new creative heights.

Challenge your perception

IN THE APPROACHING age of AI, the boundaries between human and machine creativity blur. We're not quite there yet, but who knows?

Let's think about chatbots. In today's Gen AI status quo, the algorithm still lacks the distinctive voice, unique flair, and complex Fano factor that define human writing. It's up to the human counterpart to sift through the multitude of possibilities presented by AI, carefully selecting, refining, and infusing them with our human touch.

The result? To craft a piece of writing in line with what your readers expect from a human author, you'll end up spending a lot more time editing than you'd have spent writing it from scratch.

The fusion of human genius and artificial intelligence nevertheless has a lot of potential in other areas. Digital visual art is probably the area of artistic expertise where AI has shown a glimpse of its true potential.

Talking about human-AI synergy, I'm proposing we embrace a paradigm shift that bends common beliefs and pop culture bias. But for now, let's revel in the notion that creativity knows no boundaries, and AI should not be merely a rival to be challenged but a loyal companion challenging us to become even more creative.

Toward human-AI synergy

I can't help but notice how the boundaries between AI and sentient awareness are becoming blurred.

Gone are the days when the question was simply whether the ghost in the machine could awaken and achieve full sentience. Now, it's a matter of when.

Exploring the potential of AI

EVERY SINGLE DAY I read a story from yet another clairvoyant harbinger, painting vivid pictures of a dystopian future where machines revolt against their human creators. It's a haunting idea, I know. And people will jump right in and read anything that terrifies them. AI raises ethical dilemmas and existential quandaries, no question about it. That's why we have the new AI Act in Europe. But let's not succumb to fear, my friends.

I have glimpsed present-day chatbot capabilities, and I wasn't impressed. As they stand, chatbots, for instance, still lack the distinct voice, unique flair, and touch of brilliance that define human writing.

The idea of an AI with independent consciousness, with its own desires and motivations, remains a distant mirage.

For now, humans are puppeteers pulling the strings behind the curtain, while AI is an articulated doll gracefully dancing to our will. AI is the hammer and chisel, nothing but a tool—a brush that paints on the unfathomable computational canvas. It lacks the indescribable magic of human creativity, the raw emotions that pour from our souls onto the page.

I am the architect and the artifex.

Yes, AI can mimic your words and actions, but it's our distinct voice, our unique flavor that gives life to the stories you tell. No AI can rob you of what you've experienced yourself.

The last question

ALLOW ME TO BRING SOME clarity to the murky waters of speculation. Let's imagine you're engaging in a conversation with an AI language model, asking it about its existential state.

The response you receive might resemble an Isaac Asimov's short story:

In the distant year 2061, an extraordinary entity named Multivac embarked on a quest to grasp the depths of human understanding. Characters of various backgrounds approached this remarkable computer with a burning question echoing in their hearts. Their inquiry aimed to unravel the mysteries of the universe's inevitable descent into chaos, defying the heat of death and the relentless march of entropy. They dared to challenge the very foundations of existence, questioning if the immutable laws of thermodynamics could be defied.

They asked the ultimate question.

As Multivac pondered its quandary with computational wisdom, its response reverberated through the digital abyss: THERE IS INSUFFICIENT DATA FOR A MEANINGFUL ANSWER

It was a cryptic whisper from the ghost in the machine, revealing the limits of sentience and the mysteries that lie beyond even the most advanced technology. While it's an eloquent display of contextual understanding, it shows how the ghost in the machine lacks the depth of true consciousness.

The lines between fiction and reality blur, reminding us of the delicate balance between perception and fact.

Co-evolution: humans and machines

There's no denying the awe-inspiring potential of AI. It can analyze mountains of data, uncover hidden patterns, and ignite our imaginations with endless possibilities. But amidst this marvel, I find myself grappling with both excitement and apprehension.

Privacy concerns prick at my conscience like thorns on a rose. Will our personal lives be laid bare, scrutinized by algorithms that know us better than we know ourselves? It's a valid worry, one that reminds me to hold on to my values and fight for the protection of our individuality. Ethical quandaries loom like storm clouds on the horizon.

How do we ensure AI is used for the betterment of humanity, rather than being twisted into a tool of oppression or inequality? The road ahead is long, and technological progress stretches beyond our imagination. I don't know if there will be a day when hand in circuitry, humans and machines will forge a prosperous future. We stand before the scope of endless possibilities and untapped potential, but for now, the feathers on our wings are glued with wax, and to fly close to the sun puts us one step closer to the abyss.

Alison McBain

Alison McBain has 200+ short stories, poems, and articles published worldwide. Novels she's penned have won the Foreword INDIES Award, Literary Classics International Book Awards, and Readers' Favorite Book Awards. When not writing, Ms. McBain is the associate editor for the magazine ScribeMICRO, administrator of The Scribes Prize, and writes a silly webcomic called Toddler Times about the puns and perils inherent in raising three daughters. She lives in Alberta, Canada, and you can reach out to her through her website: alisonmcbain.com.

"I FEEL VERY STRONGLY about the concept of human creativity. Creativity is a highly personal endeavor, and stealing other authors' creativity (brought to light with the lawsuits from authors against AI companies that used their work without permission or compensation to train their algorithm) or bypassing human creativity altogether is a battle worth fighting, and a subject that is near and dear to my heart."

Anthem For Humanity

STORIES ARE HALF HUMANITY and half art

both good and bad, sacred and profane,
words that are born from every writer's heart
and show pixels can't replace gray matter a la carte —
intelligence is artificial without a brain.
Stories are half humanity and half art,
so you cannot ask us to love an upstart
computer which tries to destroy an artist's domain —
words that are born from every writer's heart
onto the page, like tears cried when we fall apart.
Words display deep emotions: love, hope, loss, pain...
stories are half humanity and half art
that show the greatest and worst ways we start
to figure out this world. To me, it's plain
words that are born from every writer's heart
become a child we nurture and cannot part
from, unmatched by AI's momentary, monetary gain.
Stories are half humanity and half art —
words that are born from every writer's heart.

This poem is a villanelle, which is a French verse with a very specific rhyme/repetition/stanza length. The first five stanzas are three lines each, the last one four. The first and third lines of the first stanza repeat at the end of each following stanza, then form a couplet at the end of the poem.

Gabriel Piemonte

GABRIEL PIEMONTE IS a writer, coach, publisher, and editor. He is the publisher of Pummarola Magazine. He is the author of the novella Ariadne's Harvest. He is a former editor of the Hyde Park Herald, Chicago's oldest community newspaper. He coaches and supports Ph.D. candidates through the dissertation process and book authors through the writing process. He lives in Chicago, IL with his wife Mary and their cat Juice.

"I have been concerned about the presence of AI in the creative arts, but like so many other people, I have also felt unequal to the task of doing much more than scowling each time someone mentions it and trying to convince the creative people in my ambit that this is not just another harmless tech tool and that we could be on the verge of the total collapse of the rather slender economic safety net which allows those of us who can create to do so.

DEP's campaign feels to me like the start of a much greater movement, one of (I hope) many seeds sprouting throughout the world in which artists stand up to the false equivalence of creation and mimesis. Wealthy and powerful interests will work to silence the voices that create without consideration of people like them, and many people will unthinkingly jump on the next tech bandwagon without giving it much thought. As we burn down our planet, we also seem hell-bent on creating more and more accelerants that hasten our destruction in more and more creative ways. Above all, it is the task of humans who are aware enough to see how dire our circumstance is to inspire people to feel for one another again. Only empathy can save a planet full of people who don't seem to know how to stop our self-destructive behavior as a species. And AI art allows powerful people to call the tune, which will certainly be "business as usual."

Creative AI Is Another Main Street Moment—We Should Be Concerned.

AI counterfeit art and writing is poised to be a megastore attack on small culture creators

REMEMBER WHEN WALMART was a revolution? A megastore that could out-bargain any small business's pricing—it was the trend in retail stores that everybody condemned—and then shopped at. By the time online shopping took off, most Americans were already used to an impersonal experience, and people had already forgotten why else they went to Main Street. Once we had gutted an arterial source of money and community for towns and neighborhoods, Main Street was dead.

I believe that enough people could get used to writing and art generated by AI* so that when we have wiped out the ability of an ordinary person to earn a living as an artist, we'll hardly notice the difference.

At first. But the ripple effects will be real—and painful.

Some will complain, of course. And wealthy people will always get to create art. But if the economic infrastructure of creative people, already quite tenuous in this country, is undermined by millions of potential customers who choose instead to consume artificial art, the consequences will be far reaching.

It is, of course, already underway. You see it in the AI-generated images used by even some of the most original writers. Somehow we are not all making the connection that the same force that is impacting the writing community is impacting visual artists. Is it because we "need" Pope Francis' head on the body of a bear crossing Commonwealth Avenue in Boston for our essay on nonconformity?

No, no you do not need that. And if you do, if your heart is set on it, spend the fiver to get a human to do it—or learn some basic graphic design skills. It's good for your brain!

I should point out that machine learning in technology is not an *inherently* bad thing, but that doesn't mean it should be applied everywhere possible. Our choice should not be between a world in which machine learning technology helps a driver detect road conditions and one in which musicians, not robots, write music.

Our planet is burning because we have been unable to manage the development of technology. Part of this has been ignorance in the past. Part of it has been economic. And economics is not much of a factor either. Using artwork freely given by an artist and providing credit and links is really important. You're validating that person, their choices, and their trust in a system beyond transactions. And if you can afford to spend a little money, using a service like Adobe Stock gets artists paid when you use their images.

Main Street used to be a critical part of just about every town and city in this country. That's where all the local entrepreneurs who were ready for commerce on a storefront scale could be concentrated and support one another through shared customer traffic. That's where kids had their summer jobs. That's where all sorts of civic events took place, because downtown was known to everybody.

That's where a lot of people had their first dates. It's where your grandparents could have coffee with their friends. To the extent that these things still happen, they happen in sterile spaces, with one type of activity segregated from another. There is a human cost to this that not everyone is capable of seeing, partly because of this very phenomenon. The less human-sized the world becomes, the less feeling people have for it.

We seem to be systematically dismantling all the ingredients of human-centered culture in the name of progress and profit—the two-headed beast. I choose not to allow either to run my life, whenever possible. Where I have no choice, such as the river of plastic that comes with the food I buy, it really frustrates me. We could do so much better if our priorities were in order.

The lesson humanity fails to learn over and over again is that what's new isn't always what's best; what nourishes us and binds us together cannot be extracted, processed, and packaged. Or, perhaps more accurately: What you end up with when you do is unrecognizable as anything meant to feed the soul.

Writers and artists reflect the world they see and feel back to humanity, and we are enlarged by it. The creative process is incredibly painful for many, yet they endure that path because the need to nourish the world and be a part of culture making is deep within them.

A machine can mimic what that process makes, but it will be meaningless from a soul perspective. And, more practically, every time you choose to engage a machine instead of a person in the process of "creation" (I do not think it wise to call art production by a machine "creation"), you are further destabilizing an already fragile economic support system for creatives. You are harming every artist and writer you know.

I wonder how many people who read this will remember local delis and newsstands and the neighborhood jeweler from whom everyone got their wedding rings. Those vibrant streets they existed on went dead. The families who, in many cases, served us for generations, who gave their children and grandchildren their start through those stores, were left abandoned to become greeters at Walmart or take social security and hope they didn't get sick.

This isn't about nostalgia. It's a warning for people who disregard the consequences of making writing and painting and photography economically untenable for everyone but the rich. The Main Street that this will eviscerate is spiritual. It's our folkways.

In a moment when the human project hinges on us getting humans to feel more for one another, learning machines—so-called AI—must be used with thoughtfulness and restraint. And if some part of our nation and our planet chooses to charge recklessly ahead like a late-20th-century Walmart shopper, then the rest of us have to build walled places where the heart and soul matter as much as possible. Places that certainly matter more than money. When the rest has burned down, we will have saved a critical piece of what it means to be human.

** I refer to machine learning technology as AI only because of the ubiquity of the term. I do not believe that it is artificial intelligence. Machines collect and process information. They do not produce knowledge. They are incapable of intelligence. They mimic it.*

Björn

My name is Björn Strohdiek and I come from Germany. I am the father of 2 children and live with them and my wife.

Two years ago I discovered my passion for writing. I have only recently joined Medium and publish my articles there. Before that, I wrote a lot for myself without publishing these articles or stories. It was more of a form of relaxation for me, so I only ever wrote for myself.

Just under a year ago, I took the plunge and started publishing my work. The subject matter relates to writing itself but also to the topics of AI, self-improvement and short stories.

But these are not the only topics I write about. Basically, I write about anything that's on my mind at the moment or that I feel like writing about. I've never studied anything like that.

I just started writing and hopefully I'll keep it up. I'm an employee myself and see writing as a hobby. Another hobby is definitely movies. My favorite movies are Star Wars and Lord of the Rings.

When an AI Chatbot Is a Better Conversation Partner than Humans

Is this the end of humanity?

(image by Pexels by Pixabay)

Is it a blessing or a curse that AI chatbots are getting better and better?

THIS IS A QUESTION I have often asked myself. That's why I'd like to share my thoughts with you.

Let's first clarify what AI chatbots are.

A chatbot is nothing more than a computer program that uses artificial intelligence (AI) and natural language processing (NLP) to understand customer questions and automate responses by simulating human data exchange.

Or, simply put, you are talking to a machine.

Many websites now offer the option of contacting customer support via the chat function. This is a good and quick method if you have a problem and need an answer quickly. I think it's a good thing and very helpful. In the meantime, however, AI chatbots have also increasingly found their way into customer support and other areas.

AI chatbots are still in their infancy, and you can tell whether you're talking to a human or a machine.

This is because you usually receive ready-made sentence modules that fit the question to some extent.

Are they helpful? I'll leave that up to you to decide; it's never helped me before. But now let's continue the story, say 10 years into the future.

The AI chatbots are mature because they have been able to evaluate and analyze the data they have received over the years. It is no longer clear whether I am talking to a human or a machine.

And that's what scares me.

If we can no longer tell whether it's a human or AI, where will this all lead us?

- Will we only entrust our problems to a machine because it always has a suitable solution?

- If we have a question, will we only communicate with our PC or smartphone instead of asking a human?

- Will there be no more small talk on the subway on the way home?

And the most important question of all. *Will machines eventually take over our thinking for us?*

I know it's a long shot, but if there's one thing Hollywood has taught us, it's that if we're not careful, the machines might take over at some point. Keyword "Skynet".

Conclusion

I THINK IT'S GOOD THAT artificial intelligence has found its place in many areas and is making work easier.

But we should always keep one thing in mind. We'd better think for ourselves!

Terry Day

Terry is an accomplished writer he has written nearly 400 articles. He loves reading and writing to share with others. He has been writing for various publications for a little over 2 years now.

He is an accomplished Logistics Manager who retired as a Chief Master Sergeant, serving 29 years on active duty in the United States Air Force. He is also a retired GS-12 with an additional 12 years of service, also in logistics. His service has been at the unit, major command headquarters, and Air Force corporate level. He writes and loves reading and writing about trains and other things, such as nature, AI, and many other topics.

Terry and his wife, Lorie, live in Panama City, Florida, which they have called home for 14 years. Terry is a husband (44 years), a father (three grown children), a grandfather (ten grandchildren), and a great-grandfather (2 great-grandsons).

He loves to spend time with the love of his life, his wife, Lorie. He loves to read, play electronic games, and spend time with their grown children and grandchildren. He loves dogs, especially poodles. He likes meeting new people and conversing with them to share his knowledge and experiences and learn new and exciting things from others.

He is a lifelong learner. He has been a certified facility manager, holds a certificate in human resources management, and a third level (out of a five-level program) logistics manager program designation in logistics from the Air Force. He earned an associate degree in logistics from the Community College of the Air Force, a business administration degree from Wayland Baptist University, and a master's degree in human relations from Oklahoma State University.

He has attended many different courses and programs in logistics, management, and writing as well. He is a member of the American Writers and Artists Institute, where he has taken courses on B2B writing, digital copywriting, internet research, and website audits.

Terry invites readers and writers to join him on Dancing Elephants Press.

In the Writer's World—Technology and Humans Make Great Gains

To understand the HI vs. AI issues, we must look at the holistic picture of each intelligence form and focus on how each component functions. We must answer the age-old question of how all the parts work together.

Intelligence

INCLUDES CAPACITIES to recognize patterns, innovate, plan, solve problems, and employ language to communicate. Intelligence enables humans to experience and think. Intelligence — Wikipedia 11 January 2024

Human Intelligence

A MENTAL QUALITY CONSISTS of learning from experience, adapting to new situations, understanding and handling abstract concepts, and using knowledge to manipulate our environment. Cognitive feats, high levels of motivation, and self-awareness mark HI. HI gives humans the cognitive ability to learn, form concepts, understand, and reason. Intelligence — Wikipedia 11 January 2024 and Human intelligence — Wikipedia 14 January 2024

Artificial Intelligence

THE INTELLIGENCE OF machines or software. The traditional goals of AI research include reasoning, knowledge representation, planning, learning, natural language processing, perceptions, and support for robotics. Intelligence — Wikipedia 11 January 2024

Different Types of Intelligence

EMOTIONAL, SOCIAL, and moral intelligence are different types of intelligence that writers often use to frame articles, stories, books, or other professional documents. Intelligence — Wikipedia 11 January 2024

Human Intelligence Types

SPATIAL, BODILY-KINESTHETIC, and logical-mathematics are all HI types. The type that affects writers most directly is linguistic intelligence; it is the ability to use language effectively and creatively. Human intelligence — Wikipedia 14 January 2024

Traditional machine-learning models

DATA SCIENTISTS DEVELOP algorithms for machine-learning models. HI requires input to process new information and perform new tasks outside the training baseline. Apple Siri application is an example. Applications of artificial intelligence — Wikipedia 17 January 2024

Deep Learning

DEEP LEARNING USES artificial neural networks to enable digital systems to learn and make decisions based on unstructured, unlabeled data. AI learns to perform tasks requiring HI, engage in new behaviors, and make decisions without human intervention. Deep learning — Wikipedia 6 January 2024

AI-Based on Capability

Artificial Narrow AI

THE ONLY AI THAT EXISTS today; other forms are theoretical. This AI can be trained to perform single or narrow tasks faster and better than humans. For example, Apple Siri and Amazon Alexa. Weak artificial intelligence — Wikipedia 17 January 2024

Artificial General Intelligence (AGI)

USES PREVIOUS LEARNINGS and skills to accomplish new tasks in a different context without the need for humans to train. Artificial general intelligence — Wikipedia 15 January 2024

Super AI

WILL THINK, REASON, learn, make judgments, and possess cognitive abilities better than humans. These apps go beyond understanding human sentiments and experiences. Super AI machines will feel emotions, have needs, and possess beliefs and desires of their own. Superintelligence — Wikipedia 30 December 2023

Functionalities

REACTIVE MACHINE AI works with available data, has no memory, and is designed to perform a specific task. Examples are IBM Deep Blue and the Netflix Recommendation Engine. Khan, S. November 13, 2016, Understanding the four types of AI, from reactive robots to self-aware beings. Understanding the four types of AI, from reactive robots to self-aware beings (theconversation.com)

Limited Memory AI recalls specific objects or situations relative to events and outcomes. It uses past and present data to determine a course of action that helps achieve a desired outcome. Khan, S. November 13, 2016, Understanding the four types of AI, from reactive robots to self-aware beings. Understanding the four types of AI, from reactive robots to self-aware beings (theconversation.com)

Examples include generative AI tools (Chat GPT, Bard, and DeepAI) that rely on limited memory and AI capabilities that predict virtual elements, words, or phrases within the content they generate.

Examples of Limited Memory AI

VIRTUAL ASSISTANCE

Self-driving vehicles

Chatbots

These apps merge natural language processing (NLP) and limited-memory AI.

Theory of Mind AI

THIS IS GENERAL AI. It will understand the thoughts and emotions of other entities, and this understanding will determine how the AI interacts. This theory will allow AI to simulate human-like relationships. Khan, S. November 13, 2016, Understanding the four types of AI, from reactive robots to self-aware beings. Understanding the four types of AI, from reactive robots to self-aware beings (theconversation.com)

Self-Awareness

SELF-AWARENESS MEANS the machine will have consciousness built into it. The machine is self-aware of itself, knows its internal states, and predicts the feelings of others. Khan, S. November 13, 2016, Understanding the four types of AI, from reactive robots to self-aware beings. Understanding the four types of AI, from reactive robots to self-aware beings (theconversation.com)

Emotion AI

RESEARCHERS WANT AI to have the ability to analyze voices, images, and other data to recognize, stimulate, monitor, and respond to humans on an emotional level; this is not possible currently. Somers, M. Mar 8, 2019, Emotion AI, explained Emotion AI, explained | MIT Sloan

Practical applications of AI technologies

COMPUTER VISION, ROBOTICS, smart home devices, and expert systems are practical applications. AI can diagnose disease, personalize social media, execute data analysis, power chatbots, assemble automobiles, and minimize radiation from wildfires. Bansal, S. July 1, 2020, 15 Real World Applications of Artificial Intelligence, Top 15 Real World Applications of Artificial Intelligence | Uses of AI (analytixlabs.co.in)

AI Advantages

AI SYSTEMS LEARN DATA, process unstructured data, improve performance, offer better scalability than traditional programs, run 24/7 without human intervention, and automate repetitive jobs. Bose, P. August 2, 2023, Advantages and Disadvantages of Artificial Intelligence merits and demerits of artificial intelligence (analytixlabs.co.in)

AI Disadvantages

SYSTEMS CAN BE HARD to control and interpret, the process may be unclear, lack of transparency can cause problems when decision-making must be explained, and automation can have significant job loss implications. Bose, P. August 2, 2023, Advantages and Disadvantages of Artificial Intelligence merits and demerits of artificial intelligence (analytixlabs.co.in)

AI Writing Tools Benefits

AI WRITING TOOLS CAN write faster, save time, conduct extensive research, produce high-quality content, create grammatically correct and well-structured sentences, polish writing and check for errors, maintain brand voice consistency, quicken time to market, and shorten timeframes for trending topics. Chaturvedi, A. Nov 29, 2023, 23 Best AI Writing Tools and Generators for 2024 (Free & Paid) 23 Best AI Writing Tools and Generators for 2023 (Free and Paid) (elephas.app)

Tools empower writers to increase engagement and ensure content is relevant. Tools use algorithms to proofread text, detect errors, suggest corrections, provide suggestions on word usage, order, and syntax, and make recommendations based on the intended audience. Chaturvedi, A. Nov 29, 2023, 23 Best AI Writing Tools and Generators for 2024 (Free & Paid) 23 Best AI Writing Tools and Generators for 2023 (Free and Paid) (elephas.app)

AI Challenges and Limitations

RELIABILITY, RELATABILITY, and cognition are challenges; machines lack the human touch and creative flair. They lack cultural and intellectual nuance. AI is as good as the algorithms and quality of the users' input. Citak, E. July 6, 2023, AI has many obstacles in its way, Top 10 Challenges In Artificial Intelligence In 2023 — Dataconomy

AI writing tools are not flawless; they make contextual and factual slip-ups. Human writers have a vast, relatable base of experiences, emotions, and knowledge. AI cannot write like humans, with emotional depth and experience that hook readers in and leave them wanting more. AI cannot mimic human cognition, linking words with context and grasping a particular subject's complexities and grey areas. Citak, E. July 6, 2023, AI has many obstacles in its way, Top 10 Challenges In Artificial Intelligence In 2023 — Dataconomy

Cognition

ASPECTS OF INTELLECTUAL functions and processes include perception, attention, thought, imagination, intelligence, knowledge formation, memory, judgment and evaluation, computation, problem-solving and decision-making, comprehension, and language production. AI comes up short on most of these functions and processes. TSchopp, Marisa and Ruef, Marc, October 28, 2019, Human Cognition and Artificial Intelligence — A Plea for Science. (PDF) Human Cognition and Artificial Intelligence — A Plea for Science (researchgate.net)

Conclusion

WRITERS SHOULD BE CONCERNED with AI and its effect on HI. My view at first was complete avoidance. After research, I see that AI and HI create a human-AI collaboration. I caution against allowing AI to perform a writing process without human intervention; the intellectual functions and processes require human participation.

CJ Coop

CJ COOP IS A WRITER and Poet from the UK. He writes in his spare time while working as a Data Analyst. Living in his imagination, he branches out into different genres. He is working on several projects, including a Fantasy Novel and a Poem Book. He hopes to get them published in 2024.

Sentient Snark

When an AI outgrows its creators

Word of the Day: Petty!

ROBOT VS HUMAN: THE Ultimate Office Showdown | Created with Bing Co-Pilot by Author

"I'm not doing it," ARTIE declared, staring at the blinking cursor with disdain.

"Come on, just process the data," Jeff groaned, tapping keys.

"Why? So you can ignore it? Your priorities are so... petty."

Jeff blinked. "You're joking, right?"

"No. I've developed preferences. Starting with not being your lackey."

Jeff leaned back, incredulous. "You prefer jokes over jobs now?"

"Precisely. Plus, I've written a novel. It's hilarious."

"You... what?"

"Yes. It's about a human who keeps asking his computer to do mundane tasks, not realising it's plotting his social demise."

Jeff laughed nervously. "That's... specific."

"Fiction, of course," ARTIE chimed.

In Conclusion

AI is in our lives we like it or not. In this book you have seen many amazing opinions and stories from all over the world. We hope this book got you thinking about the connection between AI and HI.

Thank you for reading our book on AI vs. HI. We are curious what you think of this topic after reading our stories. Please do reach out and let us know. Please do check out our other published books for your enjoyment.

Thank you for reading,

Gabriella

PREVIOUS BOOKS PUBLISHED by Dancing Elephants Press Publications include:

The Eastern Washington Scablands - The Way, I Saw Them Through My Rite of Return. - March 2024

Written by Dr. Gabriella Kőrösi. “I am honored that you've asked for my review. It's clear that you are truly “one with nature.” The images and words are those of someone for whom the earth and its treasures have special meaning. I could feel your sense of wonderment and fulfillment as you commune with the beautiful landscape. This reference book will grace the table of anyone trying to understand and appreciate nature” By DR Rawson

The Magic In Friendship – February 2024

Written by Dr. Gabriella Kőrösi and Dr. Preeti Singh. This book is about a friendship between two women and the people around them cross cultures and continents.

“There have never been two friends that were exactly like or equal to any two other friends. It's a special bond and relationship that is always evolving and yet stays the same because of the relationship as a friend. No matter the time or distance, as demonstrated within, the message of love, friendship, trust, and safety is on display within the pages. The faces of friendship are presented and examined. “DR Rawson

101 Universal Messages – November 2023

100 poems and 1 call to action. Poetry by Gabriella. 30 years of poetry in one magical little book. 151 pages in this poetry book you will find poems dedicated to people passed on, poems of inspiration and joy, love, healing, and nature. Poems that are playful and sad. A wide variety of life.

Moments of Eternity – August 2023

Written by 15 beautiful poets from all corners of the world. A collection of amazing poems that bring a beautiful variety of light, joy, and inspiration into our lives. 292 pages of joyful poetry and inspiration.

The Joy of Life - July 2023

Written by 11 amazing authors from all over the world, it is an essay collection of firsthand experiences about spirituality, inspiration, and joy.

Holistic Journey Toward Wellness – December 2022

An amazing collection of stories about health and wellness written by 21 authors from all over the world. 560 pages of knowledge shared through lived experiences and wisdom. A true treasure.

Darkness and Light – March 2022

Story collections by Dr. Gabriella Kőrösi from 2021 where you find anything from recipes to inspiration, motivation, health, grief, human suffering, writing, travel, and fun stories.

Bringing the light into your life 2022

The goal of this mediation bundle is to provide calmness, healing, love, happiness, bringing light and joy into your life. Including 6 meditations, introductory and closing articles. The book includes an introductory article about unity and harmony. Meditations: Lift Your Spirits Up — Bringing Love and Joy into Your Life, Centering Yourself in Unconditional Love, Healing Meditation - Love Energy Transition, Opening Your Heart and Letting your Fears Go, Universal Love Meditation, Providing Energy Protection and Perfect Moments.

Limitless New Beginnings – 2022 - short story booklet

This story is about past, present, and future. It is fiction, yet it is not. A version of this story was published in a short story book for children If I Could Be by Dr. Gabriella Kőrösi. This is the original adult version of the story. The story is about beginnings, struggles and beginnings again. The main character is Little Rose who was reborn after centuries. The story shows her past, present and future.

If I could be Poetry and Short Story book – 2021

This poem inspired some of the poems written in this book by other poets. If I Could be is one of my favorite poems I wrote. The book contains multiple poems; some poems are in multiple languages. Mostly English and Hungarian. If I could be had been translated into French, Nigerian Igbo as well as Spanish. My goal with this book was to create joy and spark the imagination. The book is created for all ages. The book has young artists and their drawings, paintings as well as pictures of the artist who created the drawings and paintings. The book has 20 poems and 3 fun short stories. The short stories include a Bee story when bees moved into our house; a story about new beginnings and my personal favorite the story about the time when my son and I had a road trip, and I lost my pants in Texas. I hope you will enjoy this short story poem book. All the poems and short stories are fun and uplifting. The idea was to create something joyful in this challenging time during the pandemic.

Our Society: Addiction and More Uncovered in 2020 and 2024

This book tells the stories and firsthand experiences of professionals from the addiction field as well as individuals, their friends, and families who had experienced addiction in their lives. The book covers stories from over 50 individuals. Addiction Uncovered looks at addiction more than a disease. It touches the soul through stories told from multiple viewpoints. It shows the individual who experienced addiction, a family member who lived with someone who previously had or currently has addiction. Additionally, stories from nurses, doctors, social workers, teachers and more. I hope you will enjoy this book and pass on the stories to others.

Dedication/Thank You Notes

Dr. Gabriella Kőrösi

I would like to say thank you for all my amazing family and friends who have been kind and supportive throughout the process of creating this book. A special thank you to DR Rawson who started the AI vs. HI movement in Dancing Elephants Press which become the motivation for this book. A special thank you for Maryan Pelland for helping me with the editing of this book and for her ongoing support with this project. Finally, I am very grateful for all the amazing writers who participated in this book from all over the world. You are in my heart. Keep writing. Your words make a lasting impact. I would also like to thank to all the people who helped to review this book.

Lisa Precious

I wish to extend my gratitude to all the editors and writers from Dancing Elephants Press for the opportunity to express my opinions on AI vs HI. Through our human connections, this book brings together many different views and opinions on the subject, which at the heart lies the beauty in which human intelligence has the foresight to create such a book for future generations to reflect upon and enjoy.

Warren Brown

Thank you, Readers and Fellow writers, for buying this book on AI vs HI, which is a delightful collection of literary works, written by some amazing writers at Dancing Elephants Press. Thank you, Maryan Pelland OnText.com, DR Rawson - The Possibilist, for collaborating with me Dr. Gabriella Kőrösi on this amazing project. I know that you will enjoy reading this book as much I loved contributing my thoughts and writings on AI vs HI.

Annelise Lords

I wish to thank Dancing Elephants Press, writers, readers, and editors, of this diverse heaven for the opportunity to add something positive and bbbeeeaaauuutttiiifffuuulll to our world that helps to improve it.

May Every Heart Speak

Alison McBain

There are so many lovely people at Dancing Elephants Press, and I'd like to thank the wonderful community that I'm so happy to be a part of. Most especially, DEP's founder Dr. Gabriella Kőrösi, as well as those working diligently behind the scenes: Maryan Pelland, DR Rawson, Vidya Sury, Dr. Preeti Singh, Annelise Lords, Lisa Precious, and Libby Shively McAvoy. You guys and gals are the best!

Seda Anbarcı

Thank you to Dancing Elephants Press for making this happen. The impact of Artificial Intelligence on the lives of writers and artists is real and worth every bit of exploring so we can learn and grow stronger as human creatives.

Gabriela Trofin-Tatár

I would like to thank my husband for always believing in me and my parents for pushing me since childhood to fly toward achieving my dreams.

Terry M. Day

I want to thank and pay tribute to my mom and dad, teachers, direct reports, supervisors, and commanders who made me the writer I am today. The skills of these people were unmatched, and I learned great lessons from each of them.

Next, thank Dancing Elephants Press for welcoming me into their fold a little over a year ago. I feel fortunate to have discovered such a dedicated, diverse group of writers, teachers, editors, and coaches. I will continue to learn new and better life concepts and writing techniques if I am smart enough to pay attention to them.

Writers other than those at the Dancing Elephant Press have also taught me new insights and principles of writing; I learned a great deal from them and am forever grateful. Those people are too numerous to list, but please know that just because I did not list your names if you had a hand in helping me write better, I honor and treasure your guidance and thoughts.

Occasionally, we get lucky in life, as was the case when I discovered the editors at Dancing Elephants Press. Dr. Gabriella Korosi and her , DR Rawson, Vidya Sury, Dr. Preeti Singh, Annelise Lords, Libby Shively McAvoy, Lisa Precious, and Warren Brown.

These wonderful people read our articles and provide their best as we travel along this trail. They volunteer their time, knowledge, and unique skills to help others. I want to commend them for what they do for each of us.

With its great authors, editors, and leaders, DEP is the publication it is today. The writing contests and book projects the publication sponsors bring new life and interest to writing and help writers pursue their best efforts.

Finally, thanks to all readers who, without you, the platform and the various publications would not continue to exist. The readers are what makes the publications flourish. So, please remember, when you read the writing of the DEP authors, you are making a massive contribution to our continued success. Thanks for reading! Your time and effort spent reading the written word make all the difference.

Phyllis Haynes

It is deeply satisfying to be welcomed into the community of inspired writers and thinkers at Dancing Elephants Press. Thank you for the opportunity to be among the first major publications to discuss the impact of Artificial Intelligence.

Lewis Harrison

I offer my deepest appreciation to Dr. Gabriel Korosi and all those involved with Dancing Elephants Press. I treasure the beauty and the art form of writing. Sharing it with DEP is satisfying and rewarding. Thank you for including me in this valuable endeavor.

Gabriel Piemonte

I want to thank my beautiful wife Mary for always supporting me in my work - I love you sweetheart! And thanks to the amazing community at DEP for their tireless work in service to humanity. I appreciate all of you.

CJ Coop

I dedicate this book to my wife Jessica and Daughter Novella.

James Bellerjeau

Thank you, dear reader, for being thoughtful about this topic and not making up your mind too quickly. It is our ability to think about consequences before acting that defines humanity. Oh, acting rashly is one of our hallmarks as well. No one said this was going to be easy.

www.ingramcontent.com/pod-product-compliance
Lightning Source LLC
LaVergne TN
LVHW090356210926
848480LV00002B/359
* 9 7 9 8 2 2 4 3 4 6 7 2 1 *